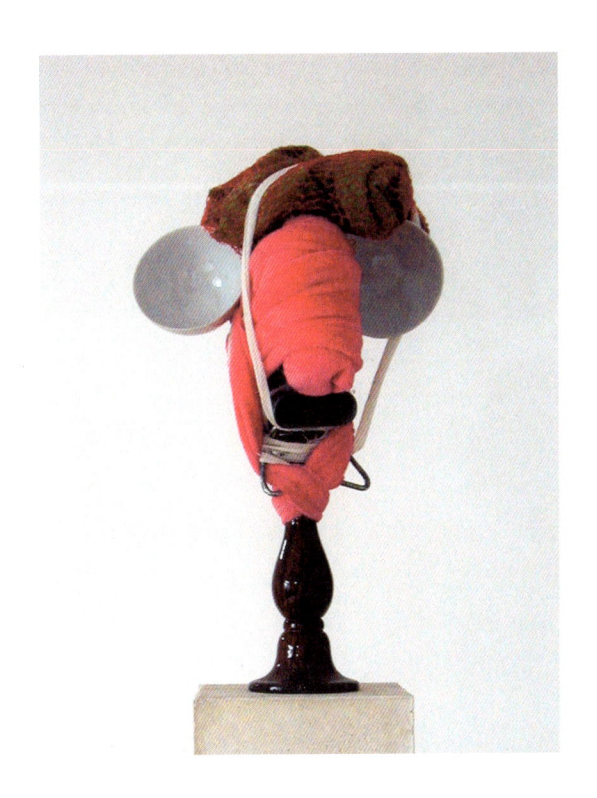

Martín Mele

Das Archiv im Wurm
El Archivo en la Polilla
The Archive in the Worm

VERLAG *für* MODERNE KUNST

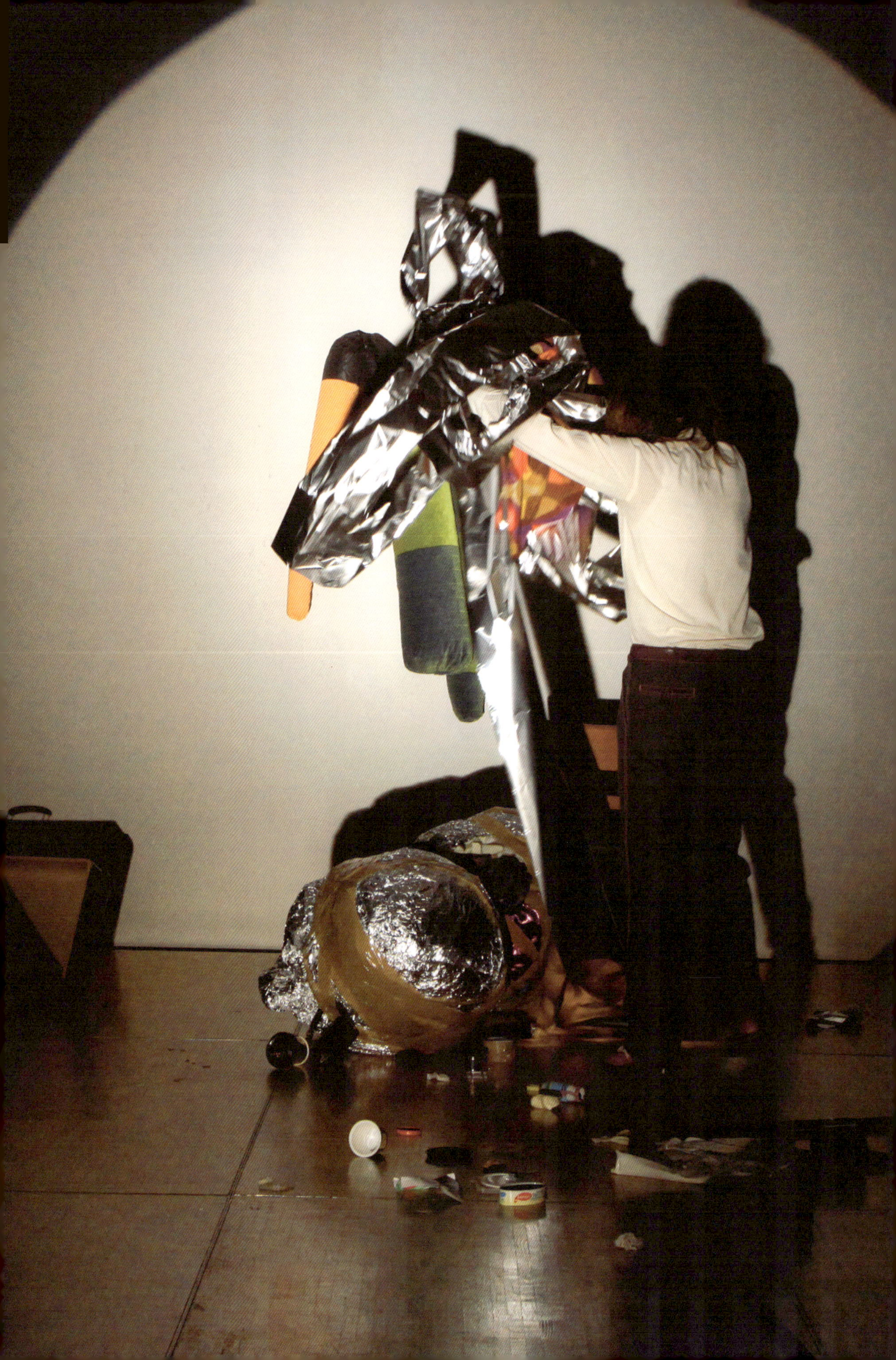

Eine biographische Notiz

Carl Friedrich Schröer

Martín Mele lebt in einem fremden Land. Wie fremd es ist, wie fern oder vertraut, weiß er nicht sicher zu sagen. Denn er lebt schon seit geraumer Zeit in der Fremde, eigentlich schon immer.

Wer wie er in Argentinien geboren ist, muss mit einer gewissen Fremdheit umgehen lernen. Zumal „als Mann, der an seine Nase festgeklebt war". Sein Vater hatte ihn spaßeshalber mit dem Poem des berühmten spanischen Dichters Quevedo vertraut gemacht und ihn so, je länger und eigenwilliger seine Nase wuchs, mit der Weltliteratur in eine besondere Verbindung gebracht.

Die Vorfahren der allermeisten Argentinier sind über das Meer ins Land gekommen. Und wollten sie wieder fort, wozu es im Laufe der Jahrhunderte wechselnde Gründe gab, mussten sie sich erneut auf ein Schiff begeben. So wurde der Hafen von Buenos Aires an der Mündung des Rio de la Plata in den Atlantischen Ozean zur Durchgangsstation der Einwanderer wie der Auswanderer, ohne dass sie sich je begegnet wären. Die Wellen der Ankömmlinge wechselten mit denen der Abreisenden, wie Ebbe und Flut. Eines Tages, als die Nase noch nicht ganz ausgewachsen war und die Welle der Auswanderer wieder einmal anschwoll, schiffte sich die Familie nach Europa ein. Ab übers weite Meer in die Fremde. Amsterdam hieß das Ziel am anderen Ende des Atlantiks.

„Das Übel", klagt der argentinische Journalist und Schriftsteller (und spätere argentinische Staatspräsident) Domingo Faustino Sarmiento in *Barbarei und Zivilisation. Das Leben des Facundo Quiroga*, ein Buch, das er 1845 im chilenischen Exil veröffentlichte: „Das

Übel, unter dem die Argentinische Republik zu leiden hat, ist ihre Weite: Allenthalben ist sie von Wüste umschlossen, und diese schleicht sich bis in ihre Eingeweide: Die Einsamkeit, die Einöde ohne menschliche Wohnstätten bildet im Allgemeinen die unerbittliche Grenze zwischen den verschiedenen Provinzen. Dort herrscht überall die Unermesslichkeit…" – Und überdies die Weite der Meere, zwischen denen die Pampa nun einmal liegt, die wochenlangen Schiffspassagen hin und her.

Der junge Mann, der an seine argentinische Nase geklebt war, wuchs also zwischen den Kontinenten auf. Spanien, wo er bei seinem Patenonkel Héctor Tizón, dem Schriftsteller und hochmögenden Verfassungsjuristen, der, wenn es politisch mal wieder brenzlig wurde, über das Meer exilierte, in die Lehre ging. Später kam er in die Niederlande, nach Amsterdam und Arnheim und schließlich, den Rhein aufwärts, nach Deutschland.

Die langen Schatten der Avantgarde im letzten Abendsonnenschein. Bezog stolz den verwitterten Neorenaissancepalast der Kunstakademie Düsseldorf am rechten Rheinufer (gar nicht weit entfernt steht das Geburtshaus von Heinrich Heine) und wusste nicht, wo ihm der Kopf stand. Lüpertz, der grandioseste Darsteller des Malerfürsten am Ausgang des 20. Jahrhunderts, wurde sein Klassenlehrer, nicht sein Meister.

Mehr da als hier und wieder hier und da. Ein Frühreisender und Spätnomade, auch er. Eigentlich eine gute Schule für eine Künstlerexistenz wie sie zum Schicksal seiner Generation wurde. Der eigenen Nase und dem Gebot des globalen Marktes folgend. Und doch kein Heimatloser und Getriebener *contre la nature*. Hatte er doch von früh an gelernt, auf so etwas wie Heimat zu verzichten, um eine eigene Person auszubilden: die schlanke, hagere Gestalt, die schulterlangen Haare, die Nase ohnehin, dazu die Tabakpfeife, die handgearbeiteten Schuhe von Correa, die eleganten Maßanzüge des Schneiders Colmenares. Derart angetan betritt er das Atelier – dass alle Pinsel, Tuben, Farbeimer, Müllwülste und Materialberge sich geschlagen geben.

Bei allem ist Martín Mele eine besondere Poesie beigegeben. Ich meine nicht, dass seine Materialcollagen, die Plastiken oder Bildobjekte, seine Installationen und Räume, auch die Malereien oder Performances literarisch in dem Sinne sind, wie Werke anderer Künstler erzählerisch und anekdotisch sind. Auch beziehen sich seine Arbeiten nicht unmittelbar auf literarische Vorlagen, noch sind es gar Illustrationen. Und doch ist ihnen das Literarische als Ingredienz und Urmelodie beigegeben, wie die surrealistische Sentenz *avant la lettre* des Francisco Gómez de Quevedo (1580–1645) von der Nase und dem Kopf, dem jungen Martín Mele die Augen nach hinten öffnete.

Die Kunst ist für ihn immer noch das fremde Land. Unermesslich und schier endlos erstaunlich, voller Neuigkeiten und Monstrosität. Immer ist die Reise ins fremde Land auch voller Irrwege und nahe dem Scheitern. Das prinzipiell Literarische seines Blicks auf die Kunst schafft eine natürliche Distanz, die das Überleben auf unsicherem Terrain sichert. Eine Unabhängigkeit, eine feine Ironie, ein subtiler Witz gelangen hier zum Ausdruck, die die Erinnerung an das Illusorische und Vergebliche,

Performance | 2006 | Galerie Mark Müller | Zürich | Switzerland

das Absurde und das Theatralische und manchmal auch Trostlose seines Tuns und seiner Existenz beinahe liebevoll wach halten.

Wie die Poesie zur schützenden Begleiterin auf seinen Schiffspassagen und Entdeckungsfahrten durch die fremden Welten geworden ist, so können wir seine Kunst aus der fremden Perspektive des Literarischen lesen lernen. Kafka, Camus und Borges als Charonisten: Wegbegleiter, Übersetzer und Fährmänner. Wir kennen das Phänomen von Radiosendungen, in denen die Interviews mit ausländischen Berühmtheiten der Musik oder Politik von den atemlosen Stimmen der Übersetzer überlagert werden. Nur für wenige Sekunden ist bestenfalls am Anfang oder Ende der Aufnahme die Stimme des Befragten im Originalton zu hören. Was aber Originalsound, was Überlagerung und Übersetzung im Werk von Martín Mele ist, das erscheint als ebenso unmöglich und müßig herauszufiltern, wie es schwer fallen dürfte, von den (zumeist europäischen) Vorfahren auf den besonderen Charakter der Argentinier zu schließen.

Das Unterwegssein als eigentliches künstlerisches Format, ein Movens und argentinisches Gebot (des Überlebens), eine Notwendigkeit. Eine Technik, die perfektioniert, dazu führt, sich ans Ziel gleichermaßen anzunähern, wie sich davon zu entfernen. Die Welt wird durchquert, ermessen und bei näherer Betrachtung als Stütze fiktionaler Begegnungen begriffen. Oder, wie Jorge Luis Borges aus seiner allumfassenden *Bibliothek von Babylon* zu berichten weiß, wie die Kunst der Kartographie einst eine solche Vollkommenheit erlangte, dass ihre beste Karte endlich selbst die Größe des Reichs erreichte und sich mit ihm in jedem Punkt deckte. Die nachfolgenden Geschlechter diese aber ruchlos den Unbillen der Sonne und der Winter überließen, bis nur in den Wüsten des Westens zerstückelte Ruinen der Karten überdauerten, behaust von Tieren und Bettlern.

Argentinische Birnen | 2003 | Deltawerk | Solingen | Germany

9

Una nota biográfica

CARL FRIEDRICH SCHRÖER

Martín Mele vive en un país ajeno. No puede decir con exactitud cuan ajeno es o hasta qué punto lejano o familiar, porque lleva viviendo fuera desde hace mucho tiempo, en el fondo desde siempre.

Quien como él nació en Argentina, tiene que aprender a lidiar con una extrañeza singular. Ya su padre, en broma, le había familiarizado con la poética del célebre escritor español Quevedo, y, según su nariz iba creciendo voluntariosamente, lo vinculó de una forma peculiar con la literatura universal. Así, fue rebautizado como "érase un hombre a una nariz pegado".

Los antepasados de la mayoría de los argentinos han llegado a la tierra a través del mar. Y cuando deseaban irse, porque a lo largo de los siglos tuvieron varios motivos para hacerlo, debieron volver a embarcarse. De esa manera, el puerto de Buenos Aires – en la desembocadura del Río de la Plata al Océano Atlántico – se convirtió en una estación de paso tanto para inmigrantes como para emigrantes, sin jamás encontrarse los unos con los otros. Las oleadas de los recién llegados se alternaban con las que partían, como el vaivén de la marea alta y la marea baja. Un día, cuando la nariz aún no se había desarrollado del todo y la marea de la emigración estaba nuevamente en aumento, la familia embarcó hacia Europa, a través del alta mar hacia una tierra extranjera. Amsterdam fue la meta al otro extremo del Océano Atlántico.

"El mal que sufre la argentina", se queja el periodista y escritor argentino (y más adelante presidente de Argentina) Domingo Faustino Sarmiento en *Civilización y Barbarie: Vida de Juan Facundo Quiroga*, libro que publicó en 1845 desde el exilio chileno, "es su extensión: por todas las partes está rodeada por el desierto, y éste se mete en sus entrañas. La soledad, el desamparo sin hogares humanos, en general forma la inexorable frontera entre las distintas provincias. Allí en todas partes gobierna

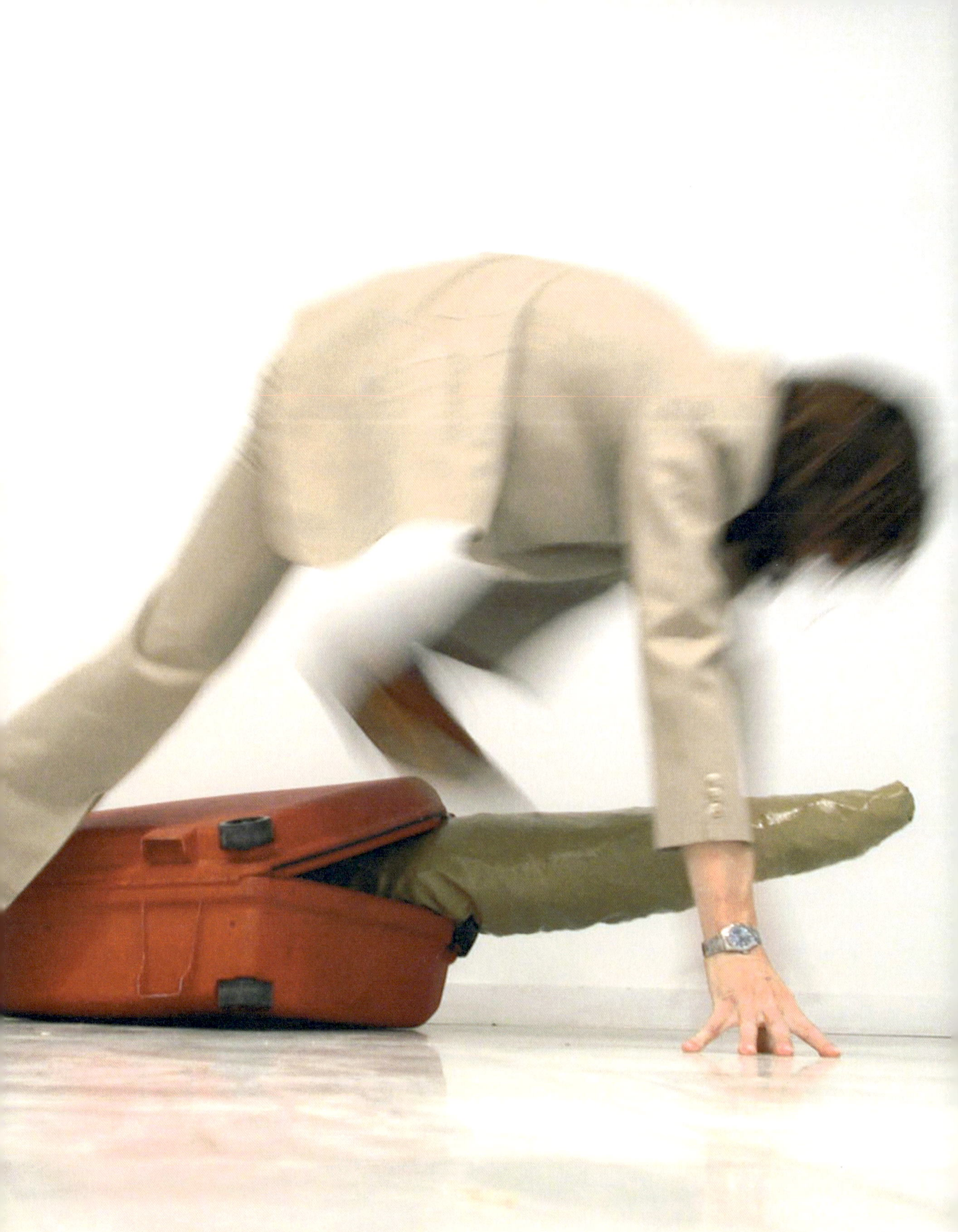

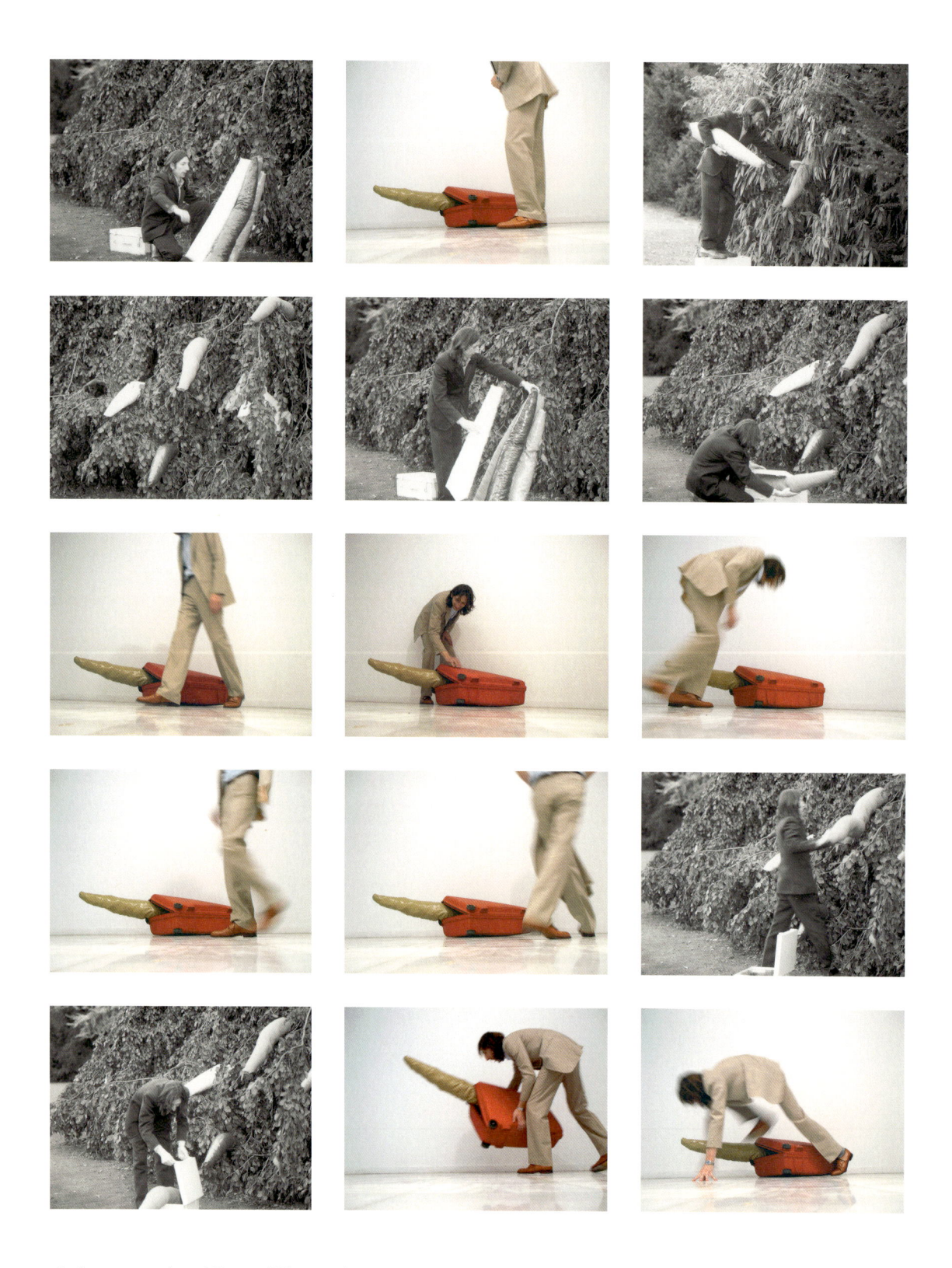

b/w: Performance | 2005 | Nordpark | Düsseldorf | Germany
color: Performance | 2005 | Sala Rivadavia | Cádiz | Spain

la inmensidad … ". Y a esto se suma la amplitud de los mares, entre los cuales se extiende la inmensa Pampa, que implican semanas de largos pasajes por mar de aquí para allá.

El joven que estaba pegado a su nariz argentina, así se crió entre los continentes. En España recibió la enseñanza de su padrino Héctor Tizón, el escritor y solemne abogado constitucional, quien cuando la situación política nuevamente se tornó demasiado arriesgada, emprendió el exilio a través del mar. Más adelante llegó a los Países Bajos, a Amsterdam y Arnheim y finalmente Rin arriba, hasta Alemania.

Pero las sombras largas de la vanguardia caen en los últimos rayos de su atardecer. Con orgullo y la cabeza hecha un lío se mudó al viejo palacio neorrenacentista de la escuela de Bellas Artes de Düsseldorf, donde muy cerca también nació Heinrich Heine. Lüpertz, el artista representante más grandioso del "Rey de la pintura" a finales del siglo XX, se convirtió en su tutor, no en su maestro.

Más allá que aquí y otra vez aquí y allá, se convirtió en viajero temprano y en nómada tardío. En el fondo, una buena escuela para la existencia de un artista, destino de su generación: siguiendo su olfato y el mandamiento del mercado global. Y, sin embargo, no siendo un sin hogar a la deriva conducido *contre la nature*. Porque él aprendió, desde muy temprana edad, a renunciar a algo como la patria para dar forma a su propia persona: de figura esbelta, flaco, el pelo largo hasta los hombros, la nariz ya de por sí evidente, además de su pipa, los zapatos hechos a mano por Correa y los trajes elegantes a medida del sastre Colmenares. Así, dotado con esas características, entra en su estudio en donde todos los pinceles, tubos, latas de pintura, y montones de material de deshechos se rinden ante él.

En todo, a Martín Mele le acompaña lo poético. No quiero decir que sus collages, esculturas y objetos pictóricos, sus instalaciones y espacios, sus pinturas o performances sean literarias en el sentido como las obras de otros artistas pueden ser narrativas y anecdóticas. Sus obras no hacen referencia directa a fuentes literarias, ni por supuesto son ilustraciones. Y, sin embargo, les acompaña el ingrediente literario y una melodía ancestral, igual que la sentencia surrealista *avant la lettre* de Francisco Gómez de Quevedo (1580–1645) sobre la nariz y la cabeza, que al joven Martín Mele le abrió los ojos para otro lado.

El arte para él aún es el país desconocido: inmenso e interminable en su capacidad de causar asombro, lleno de novedades y monstruosidades. Un viaje a tierras extrañas que también está cargado de desvíos y cercano al fracaso. Lo principalmente literario de su mirada sobre el arte consigue una distancia natural, que asegura la supervivencia sobre terreno inseguro. Aquí se manifiesta una independencia, una refinada ironía, una broma sutil que logra mantener despierto con un cierto mimo el recuerdo de lo ilusorio y lo inútil, de lo absurdo, lo teatral y a veces incluso la desolación de sus actos y su existencia.

Igual que la poesía se convirtió en compañera protectora en sus pasajes por alta mar y aventuras por mundos desconocidos, podemos aprender a leer su arte desde la perspectiva literaria ajena. Kafka, Camus y Borges como caronistas : compañeros de camino, traductores y barqueros. Conocemos el fenómeno de los programas de radio, en los que las entrevistas a celebridades extranjeras de la música o la política están sobrecargadas con las voces exhaustas de los traductores. Apenas por unos segundos, al principio y al final de la

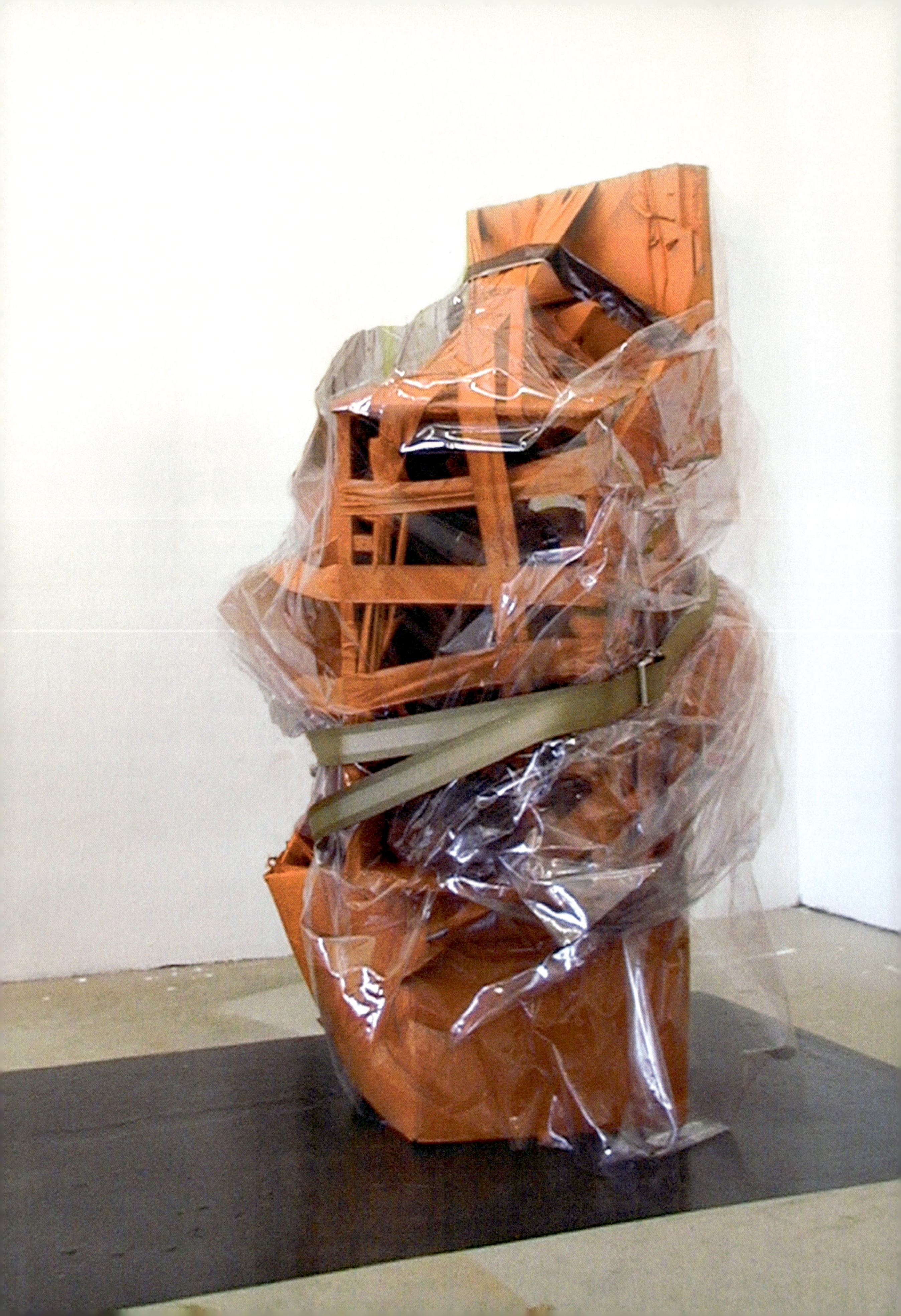

Untitled | 2000 | 140 x 60 x 70 cm (left)
Mele vs. Mele | 2007 | MACO | Oaxaca | Mexico (right)

transmisión, podemos escuchar la voz del entrevistado en su sonido original. En la obra de Martín Mele, lo que aparece como tono original y lo que es superposición y traducción, se hace igual de imposible y difícil de filtrar que juzgar sobre el carácter Argentino a través de sus antepasados (la mayoría de origen Europeo).

  El estar de viaje como formato artístico es una fuerza, un motivo y una condición argentina de supervivencia, una necesidad. Una técnica que, perfeccionada, consigue tanto aproximarse a la meta como alejarse de ella. El mundo es atravesado, medido y – cuando se analiza detenidamente – entendido como un sustento de encuentros ficticios. O, como Jorge Luis Borges nos cuenta en su colección completa *Biblioteca de Babel* que el arte de la cartografía una vez alcanzó tal perfección, que su mejor mapa, finalmente, incluso alcanzó el tamaño del Imperio y lo cubría en toda su extensión. Pero, las siguientes generaciones la dejaron expuesta a la injuria del sol y del invierno y apenas en los desiertos del oeste perduraron algunas ruinas despedazadas de los mapas, habitados por animales y mendigos.

Performance | 2008 | Langen Foundation | Hombroich | Germany

A biographical note

CARL FRIEDRICH SCHRÖER

Martín Mele lives in a foreign land, it's uncertain how foreign, how distant or familiar it is. For he has lived abroad for some time, actually forever.

Those born in Argentina have to learn to deal with a certain foreignness. Especially "as a man stuck to his nose." In jest, his father made him familiar with this poem by the famous Spanish poet Quevedo, establishing a special tie to this world literature the longer and more idiosyncratically his nose grew.

The ancestors of almost all Argentineans came to the country from across the ocean. And if they wanted to go back, for which there have been changing reasons over the centuries, they had to get on a ship anew. The harbor of Buenos Aires at the mouth of the Rio de la Plata on the Atlantic Ocean became the transit station for immigrants and émigrés without them ever meeting. The waves of new arrivals alternated with the waves of those departing, like high and low tides. One day, when the nose was not yet fully grown and the wave of émigrés swelled once more, the family boarded a boat to Europe. Across the wide ocean to foreign lands. The goal at the other end of the Atlantic was Amsterdam.

"The evil" that the Argentinean journalist and writer (and later Argentinean president) Domingo Faustino Sarmiento laments in his book *Facundo: Civilization and Barbarism*, published in 1845 in Chilean exile: "The evil that plagues the Republic of Argentina is extension: the desert surrounds it on all sides, it insinuates itself into its innermost regions; solitude, desolation without human habitation, are in general the unquestionable limits between these or the other provinces. Immensity abounds everywhere." And beyond this the expanses of the oceans between which the pampas, after all, lie, the weeks-long boat passages back and forth.

The young man stuck to his Argentinean nose grew up between the continents. In Spain, where he was apprenticed to his godfather Héctor Tizón, the writer and es-

Performance | 2008 | Langen Foundation | Hombroich | Germany (top)
Süsse Alpträume | 2008 | Field Institute Hombroich | Hombroich | Germany (right)

teemed constitutional lawyer, who went into exile across the ocean when things once more became politically dicey. Later he came to the Netherlands, to Amsterdam and Arnhem, then moved up the Rhine to Germany.

The long shadows of the avant-garde fell across the last glimmer of twilight. He proudly took up residence in the weather-beaten neo-Renaissance palace of the Kunstakademie Düsseldorf on the right bank of the Rhine (not very far from the birthplace of Heinrich Heine) and didn't know where to turn. Lüpertz, the greatest embodiment of the painter-prince at the end of the twentieth century, became his teacher – but not his master.

More there than here, and again here and there. He, too, an early traveler and a late nomad. Truly a good schooling for an artist's existence as became the fate of his generation. Following his nose and the demand of the global market. And yet not drifting without a home and *contre la nature*, for he had learned from early on to do without something like a homeland, to form his own personality. The thin, gaunt figure, the shoulder long hair, his nose in any case, and then the pipe, the handmade Correa shoes, the elegant custom-made Colmenares suits. Attired in such a fashion

19

SELF PORTRAIT | 2006 | STEFANIE AND ALFREDO HÄBERLI COLLECTION | ZÜRICH | SWITZERLAND (TOP)
GESTERN UND HEUTE | 2008 | MALKASTEN | DÜSSELDORF | GERMANY (RIGHT)

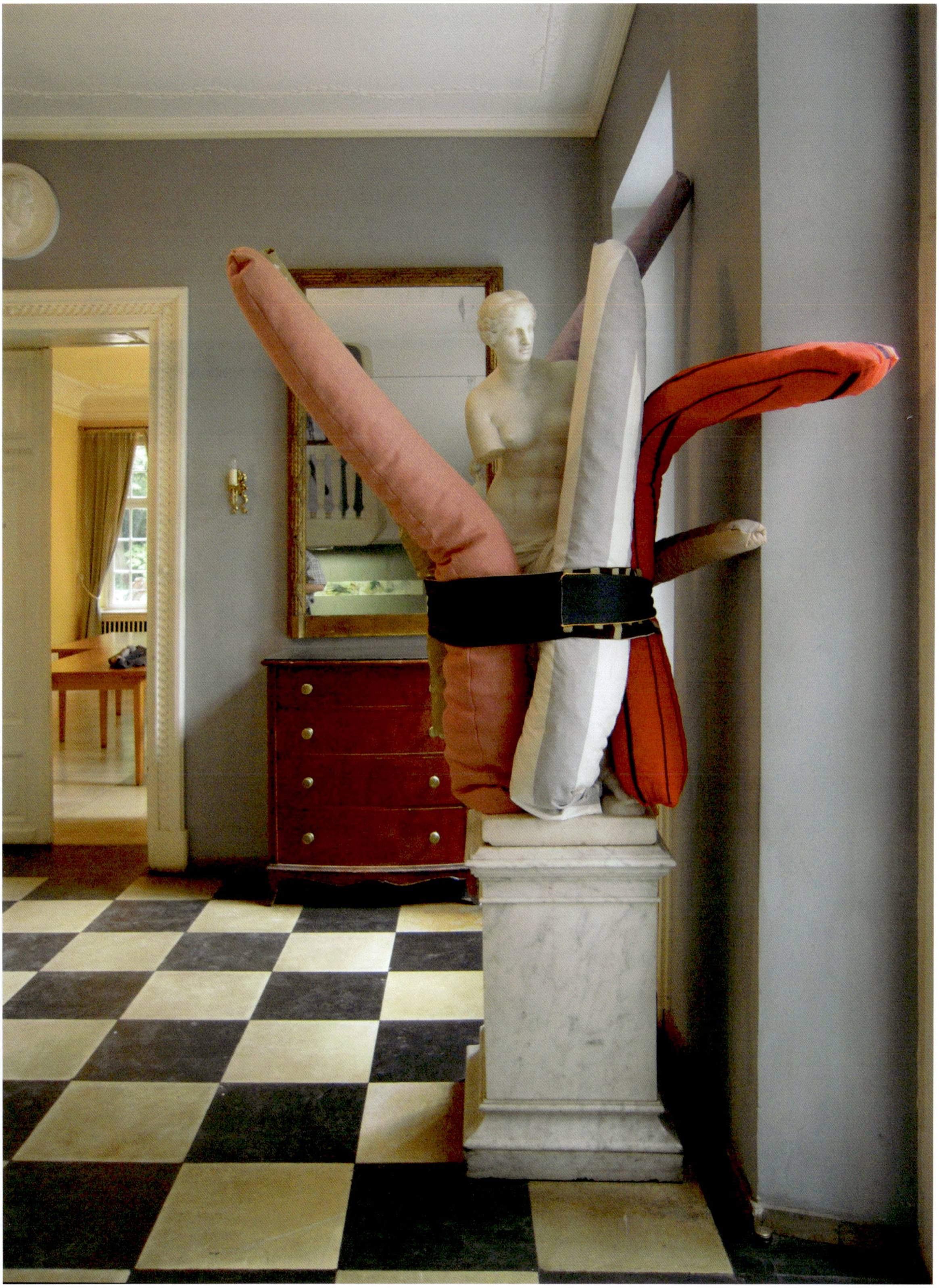

2006/2008/2006 | Galerie Mark Müller | Zürich | Switzerland (top)
2006 | Galerie Mark Müller | Zürich | Switzerland (right)

he enters the studio, causing all the brushes, tubes, paint buckets, piles of trash and material to surrender.

For everything about Martín Mele has a certain poetry. By this I don't mean that his material collages, the sculptures or visual objects, his installations and spaces, his paintings and performances are literary in the sense that works of other artists are narrative and anecdotal. His works also do not refer directly to literary models, nor are they illustrations. And yet they contain the literary as an ingredient and primal melody, like Francisco Gómez de Quevedo's (1580–1645) surrealist sentence *avant la lettre,* about the nose and head that once opened Martín Mele's eyes to the past.

For him, art remains a foreign land, immeasurable and sheer endless in its fascination, full of novelties and monstrosities. The journey to a foreign land is always full of mistaken paths and close to failure. The fundamentally literary quality of his perspective on art provides a natural distance that ensures survival on insecure terrain. An independence, a fine sense of irony, a subtle humor comes to expression, which keeps the memory of the illusory and the futile, the absurd and the theatrical, and sometimes the disconsolation of his action and his existence almost lovingly awake.

As poetry came to be a protective companion on his ship passages and travels of discovery through foreign worlds, we can learn to read from his art from the foreign perspective of the literary. Kafka, Camus, and Borges as manifestations of Charon: guides, translators, and ferrymen. The phenomenon is familiar from the radio where interviews with foreign celebrities of music or politics are superimposed with the breathless voice of the translator. We can only hear the original voice of the person at the start or the end of the recording. Yet it is as impossible and pointless to distil what is original from what is the superimposition or the translation in the work of Martín Mele, as it is difficult to deduce the special character of the Argentineans from their (usually) European ancestors.

Travelling as an artistic format of its own is a strength, a driving force and an Argentinean necessity to survive, a technique that when perfected means both approaching the goal and simultaneously moving away from it. The world is crossed, surveyed, and understood on closer inspection as a support for fictional encounters. Or, as Jorge Luis Borges knows very well from his comprehensive *Babylonian library*, the art of cartography once achieved such perfection that its best map was the size of the empire itself and covered each and every point of it. But later generations left it exposed to the scorn of the sun and the winter, until all that remained were the fragmented ruins of the maps in the deserts of the west, inhabited by animals and beggars.

Wenn ein Stuhlbein zum Rotor wird

RAIMUND STECKER

Koffer über Koffer – und Teller, Vasen, Krüge und Schalen, übereinander gestapelt, wie Kronen obenauf. Teppichrollen und Stühle, Verpackungskartons und Handtücher, offensichtlicher Abfall und Sperrmüll mit Klebeband gebunden und in Balance gebracht. Tücher, eng gespannt an Wände, unterfüttert mit dem 08/15-Campingstuhl für Binnenseesonnenfrischler, und als solche reliefartig präsent. Auf Keilrahmen gespannte Leinwände, ausgepolstert mit nicht eindeutig zu identifizierenden Gegenständen, die der geometrisch sicheren Malform zuwider streben. Hartschaumige Rüssel, gerade von den Wänden abstehend oder auch schwächelnd sich neigend, die ein Schmunzeln nicht verunmöglichen.

Dass jeder Stuhl und jede Vase, jeder Koffer und jeder Spazierstock, jede Teppichrolle, jeder Kerzenleuchter, jeder Hartschaumrest und überhaupt jedwedes Ding eine Skulptur ist dann, wenn es präsentiert wird, um unter ästhetischem Gesichtspunkt angeschaut zu werden – dies bedarf heutzutage keiner besonderen Betonung mehr. Dass oftmals eine bloße Plinthe, ein zusammengezimmerter Sockel oder auch nur der Ort der Präsentation die Funktion auszufüllen vermögen, aus einem Stuhl nicht nur eine Sitzmöglichkeit, aus einer Vase nicht nur ein Blumenbehältnis, aus einem Koffer nicht nur ein Reiseutensil, aus einem Spazierstock nicht nur eine Gehhilfe, aus einer Teppichrolle nicht nur eine Transportform, aus einem Kerzenleuchter nicht nur ein kerzenhaltendes Dekorationsmoment, aus einem Hartschaumrest nicht nur Abfall, dass also Präsentationsbesonderheiten aus allem

Untitled | 2010 | 105 x 55 x 40 cm

normal Dinglichen etwas anderes werden lassen können, hat mittlerweile mehr oder minder jedermann verstanden. Dass mithin an Orten der Kunst solche wie soeben angerissene Situationen zuhauf vorzufinden sind und noch immer zelebriert werden, verwundert nicht mehr, sondern ermüdet.

Anders verhält es sich mit den Arbeiten von Martín Mele. Er nutzt all diese alltäglich funktional bestimmten Dinge und kommt zu Collagen und Installationen, zu Environments und Reliefs, zu Situationen und Werken, halt zu Bildern und

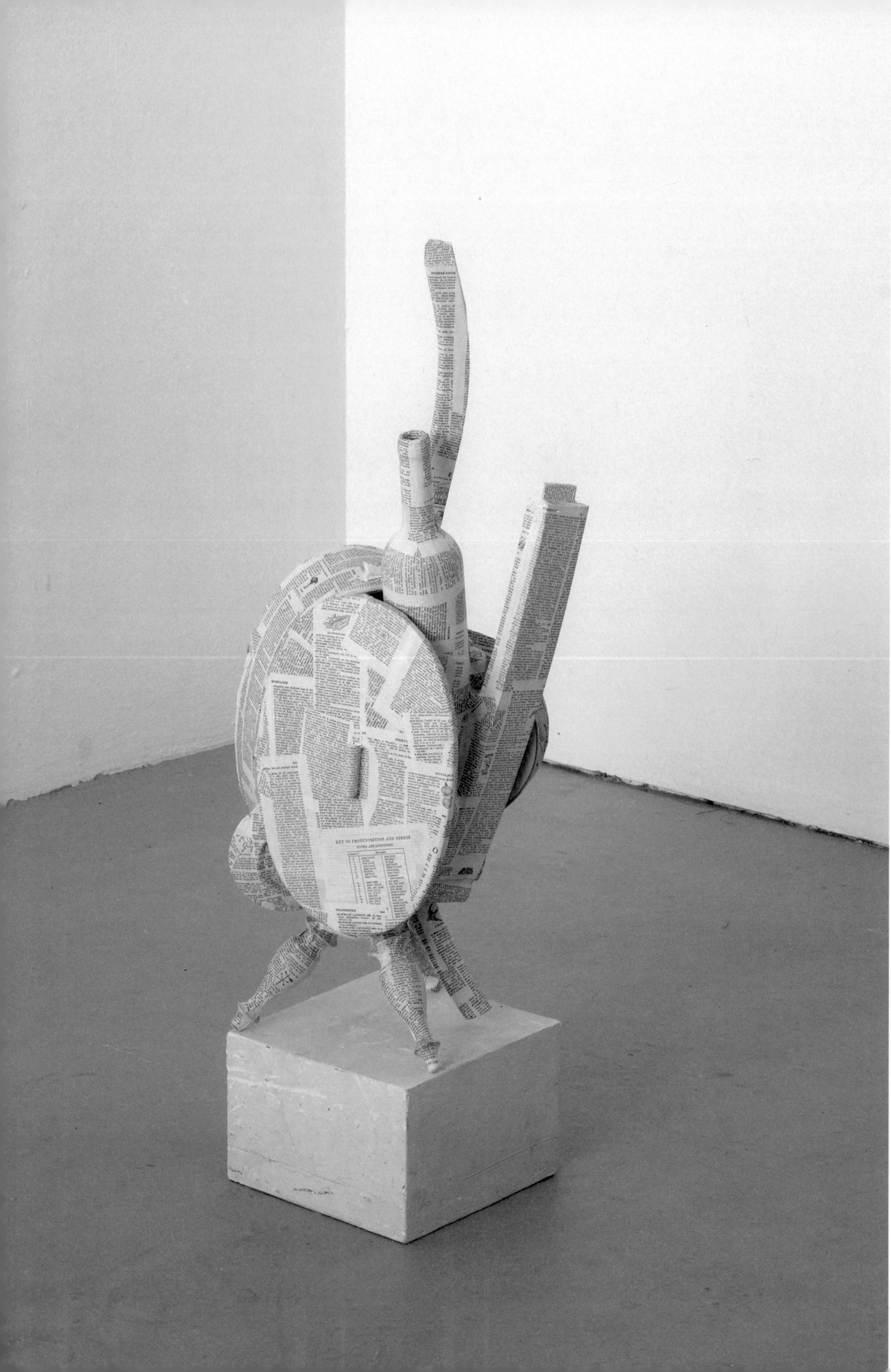
KEY TO PRONUNCIATION AND STRESS

Untitled | 2010 | 75 x 40 x 30 cm (left)
Koffer | 2009 | 40 x 72 x 42 cm | Private collection | Zürich | Switzerland (right)

Skulpturen, die schon allein aufgrund ihrer Nichtfunktionalität nur eines sein können: eben allein der ästhetischen Erfahrung überantwortete Bilder und Skulpturen.

Und was geben sie zu erfahren? Überwältigend ist das Rot oder Gold zweier Wandarbeiten, die aus gespannten Tüchern bestehen und aufgrund eingespannter Campingstühle zu Reliefs sich wölben. Die Stühle verschwinden beispielsweise hinter der roten Fläche, die vor der Wand zu schweben scheint – oder besser: die durch die eingespannten Stühle vor die Wand geschwebt zu werden scheint.

Dieses Sich-Verselbstständigen von Dingen als nahezu rein-visuelle Attraktionen scheint als ein durchgehendes Moment aus der Kunst von Martín Mele auf. Die Dinge verlieren in der Kunst Martín Meles ihre Dinghaftigkeit, obwohl das Benennen der verwendeten Dinge in seinen Werken noch kommunikatives Vehikel ist. Der Campingstuhl unter dem stramm gespannten Stoff entschwindet aber schlussendlich nahezu gänzlich als Campingstuhl. Seine durch*scheinenden* Umrisse erweisen sich in der Betrachtung des Werkes als weniger bedeutend denn die szenische Darstellung auf einer antiken Vase. Es ist ein gewölbtes goldenes Viereck, ein blau umrahmtes Gold, eine Licht reflektierende Glanzfläche, ein edel strahlendes Quadrat, das aufgrund seines Gespanntseins genau genommen gar kein Quadrat mehr ist, das an die Wand montiert, so für sich nahezu visuell autonome Präsenz einfordert. Der Stuhl verhält sich zum augenfällig präsenten Bild nur noch wie eine applizierte Szene zur ideal gerissenen Form einer antiken Vase, die lediglich auch noch Trägerin ist der Darstellung.

Es sind wirbelnde Extremitäten, Propellerflügeln gleich, die vorzugeben vermögen, um ein Zentrum herum rotieren zu können. Ein Zentrum hält sie zusammen. Textspalten von Zeitungsseiten definieren diese Mitte. Dass die Zeitungsseiten Dinge, Gegenstände umkleben und die Extremitäten die Beine und Lehne eines Stuhls sind, erweist sich – will man sich nicht mit dem einfachen Benennen von Wiederzuerkennendem zufrieden geben – als nebensächlich. Dass es sich um eine Skulptur handelt, die um ihr Gleichgewicht ringt, die gleichsam balanciert, die zu schwanken scheint und dennoch klar steht, die unvorhersehbare Dynamik in ihrer Statik zur Anschauung bringt, das scheint auch auf, ohne die Dingbezüge zu realisieren – nein, das scheint nur auf, wenn die Dingbezüge nicht im Mittelpunkt des Interesses stehen.

Martín Mele spielt dieses Spiel. Er sieht offensichtlich in Gewohntem das Auch-Andere. Er zeigt Simples und meint Komplexes. Er erkennt fraglos abstrakte Werte in Konkretem. Er scheint die Formen von Dingen nicht allein als Dingformen zu sehen, wenn er durch die Straßen zieht und Sperrmüll sammelt, wenn er sein Kunstmaterial im Trödel aufstöbert. Er erkennt unzweideutig das Abstrakte von Formen an und in den Dingen. Denn aus den von ihm verwendeten Fundstücken als skulpturale Grundlagen treten immer überdingliche Werte hervor – beispielsweise der des Stuhls, der zurücktritt hinter das Bild als Bild, das er entledigt seiner Funktion, gleichwohl mitbestimmt. Midas gleich folglich scheint Martín Mele Skulpturen und Bilder zu sehen, wo nur Material vermutet wird.

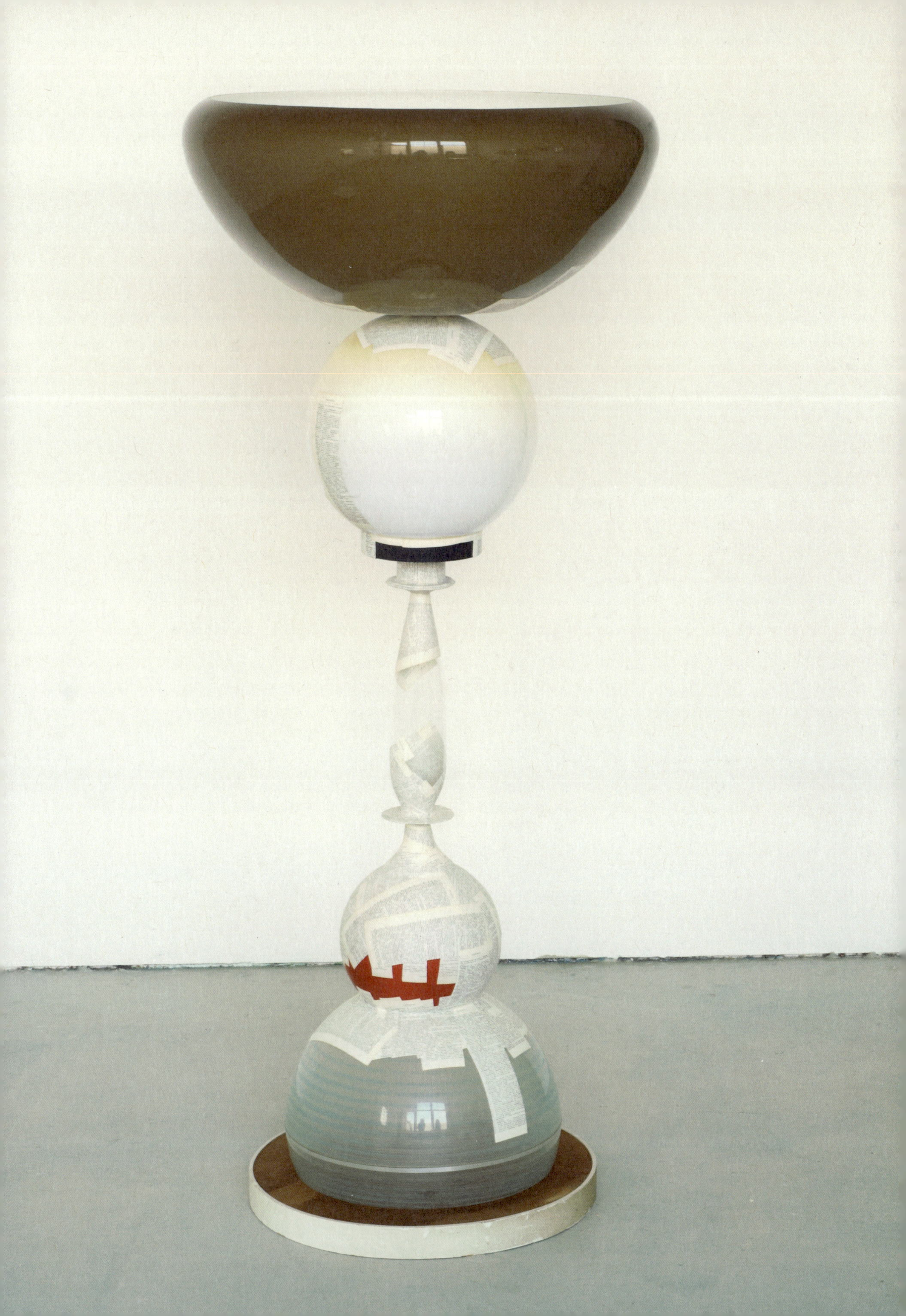

30

Untitled | 2009 | 116 x 95 x 15 cm (Left top)
Untitled | 2000 | 30 x 30 x 25 cm (Left bottom)
Netz | 2009 | 200 x 140 x 135 cm (Right)

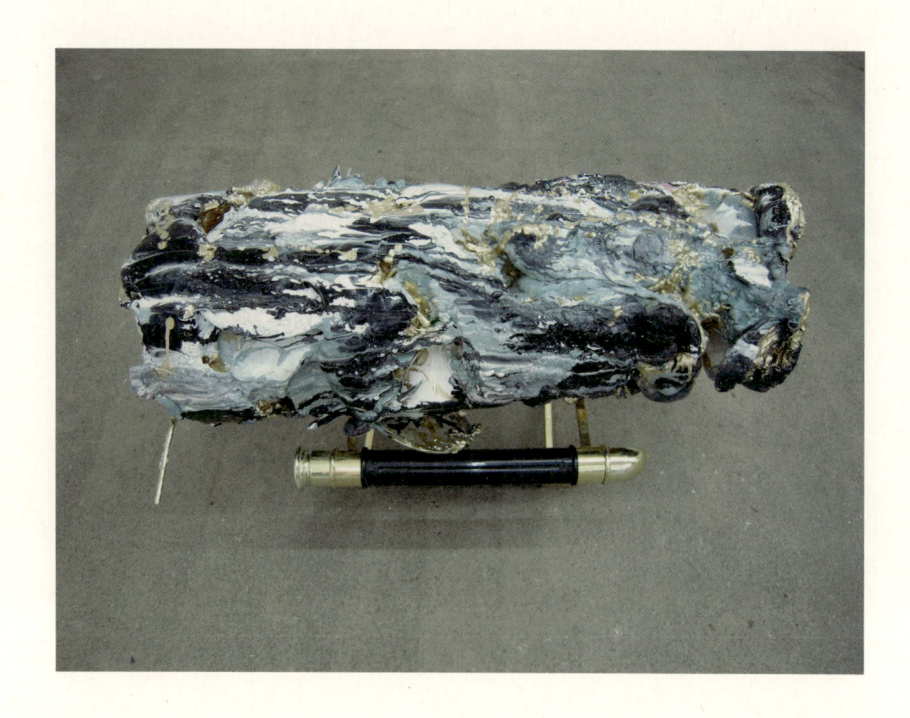

Mesa turca | 2008 | 61 x 94 x 49 cm (top)
Ecke | 2005 | 95 x 56 x 67 cm | Private collection | Zürich | Switzerland (right)

33

Untitled | 2009 | 40 x 30 x 40 cm (left)
Nasen | 2005 | 100 x 100 x 100 cm | Private collection | Zürich | Switzerland (right)

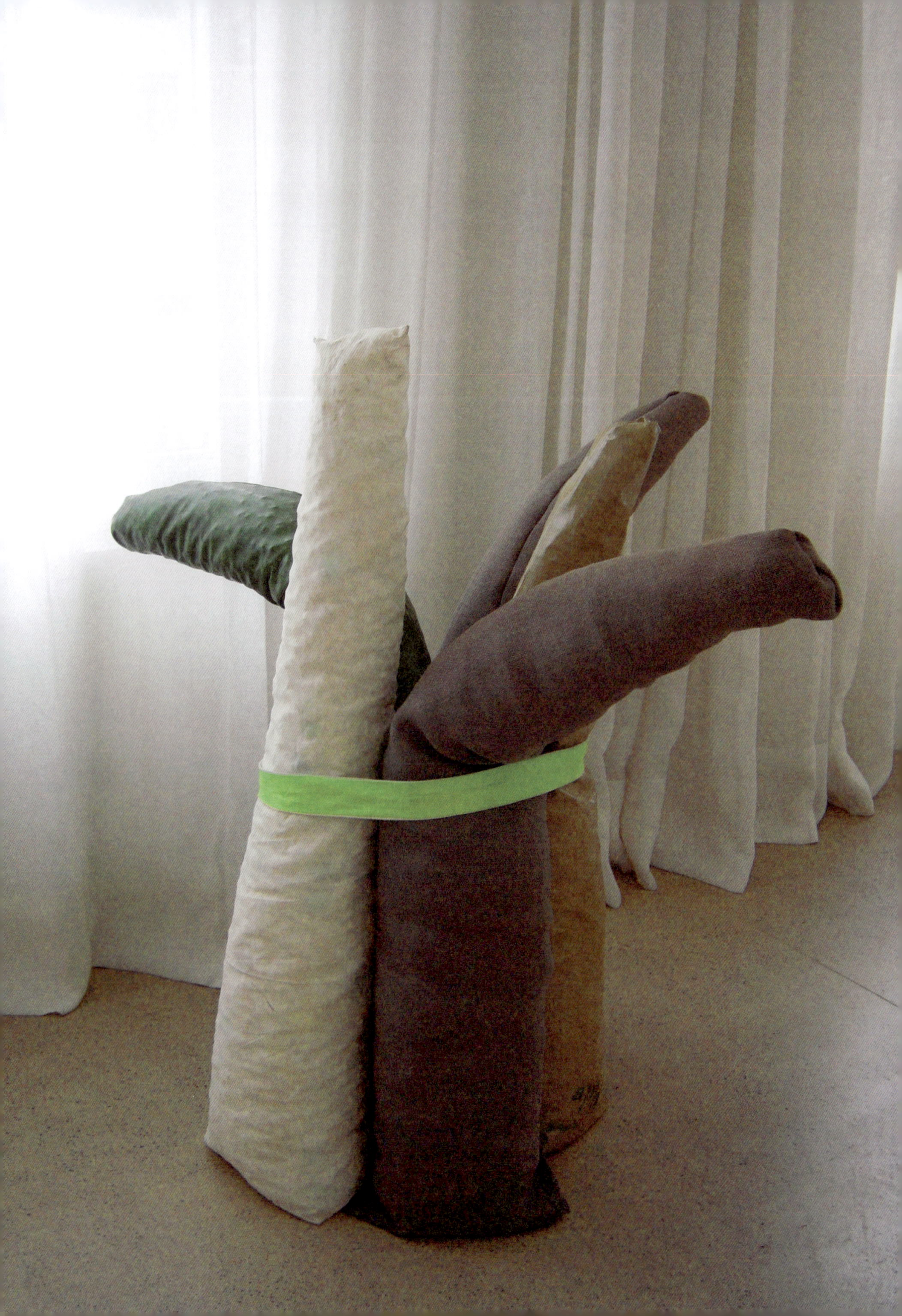

UNTITLED | 2001 | 60 x 60 x 60 cm

Cuando la pata de una silla se convierte en un rotor

RAIMUND STECKER

Maletas sobre maletas, platos, floreros, jarras y cuencos, apilados uno encima de otro cual coronas; rollos de alfombras y sillas, cajas de cartón y toallas, obvios deshechos y trastos voluminosos atados con cinta y llevados al equilibrio; telas tensadas sobre las paredes acolchadas con la silla de camping modelo 08/15 para domingueros helioxigenados y como tal, presente en forma de relieve; lienzos tensados sobre bastidores acolchados con objetos no identificables que van contra la manera segura y geométrica de pintar; trompas de espuma de poliuretano que sobresalen de las paredes o se inclinan venciéndose, ante las que se hace imposible no sonreír.

   Que cada silla y cada florero, cada maleta y cada bastón, cada rollo de alfombra, cada candelabro, cada resto de espuma de poliuretano, y en general cualquier cosa pueda ser una escultura, cuando es presentada para ser mirada, hoy en día, no requiere ningún énfasis particular. Que a menudo un mero plinto, un pedestal fugazmente carpinteado, o la ubicación de la presentación cumplan la función de convertir una silla en otra cosa que una posibilidad para sentarse, un florero en otra cosa que un recipiente de flores, una maleta en otra cosa que un utensilio de viaje, un bastón en otra cosa que una ayuda para caminar, un rollo de alfombra en otra cosa que una manera de transporte, un candelabro en otra cosa que una circunstancia decorativa con velas, un resto de espuma dura de poliuretano en otra cosa que residuo, en síntesis, el que las características de presentación puedan hacer de las cosas

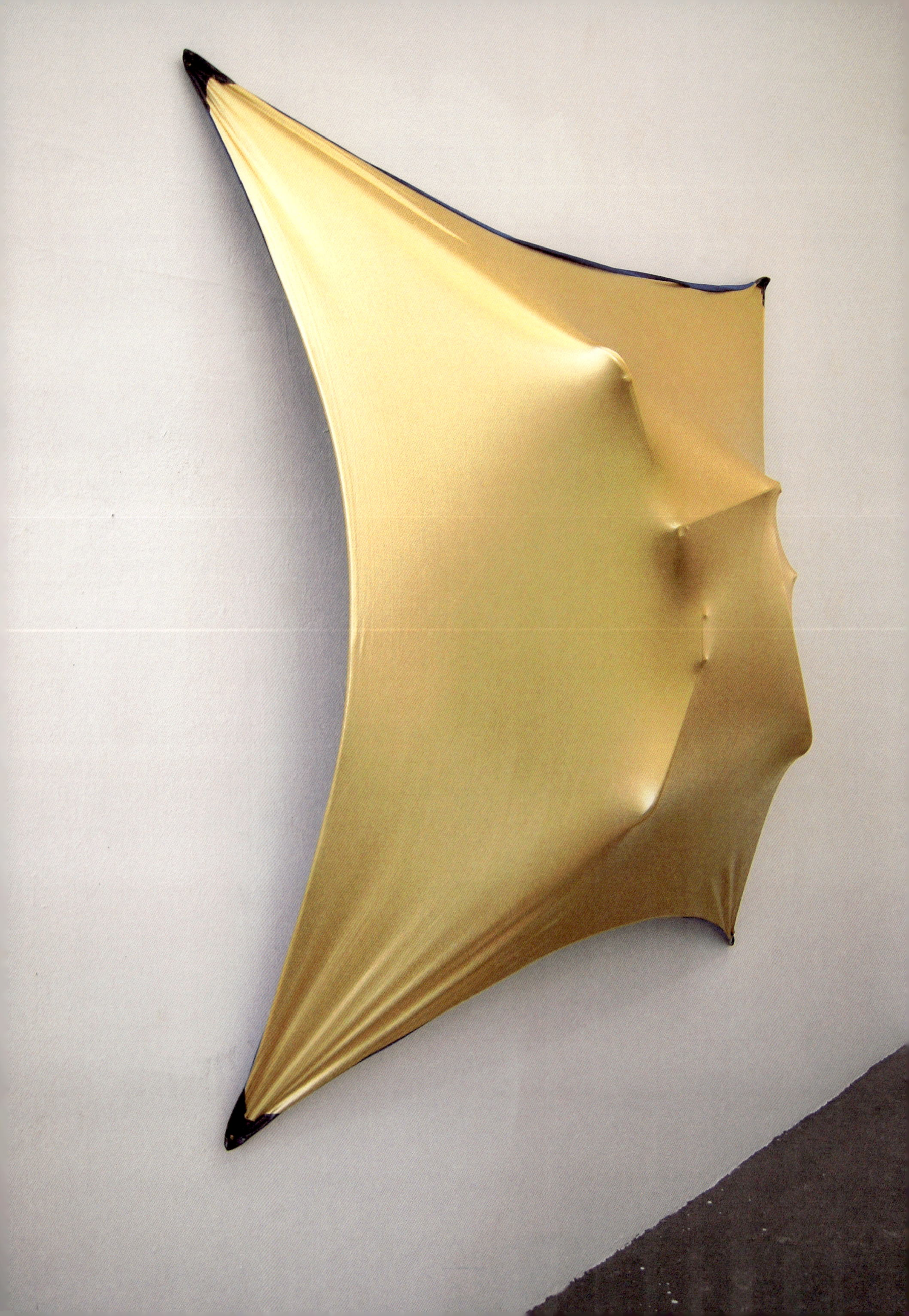

Untitled | 2003 | 120 x 40 x 40 cm | Untitled | 2005 | 60 x 120 x 40 cm (top)
Untitled | 2010 | 190 x 170 x 56 cm (left)

reales normales otra cosa, hasta hoy, mas o menos, lo ha entendido todo el mundo. Que en muchos lugares del arte aún abunden situaciones como si se hubieran comenzado en el momento y que se sigan celebrando, ya no sorprende, sino cansa.

Es diferente con los trabajos de Martín Mele. Él utiliza todos estos objetos comunes con función llegando a collages e instalaciones, a entornos y relieves, a situaciones y obras, a imágenes y esculturas, que ya por el hecho de su no-funcionalidad únicamente pueden ser eso: imágenes y esculturas que rinden cuenta exclusivamente de la experiencia estética.

Y que dan a conocer? Es sobrecojedor el rojo o el oro de dos piezas sobre la pared de telas tensadas que se abomban formando un relieve. Más aún porque las sillas desaparecen detrás de la superficie roja que parece flotar ante la pared o, mejor, que parece haber sido suspendida por las sillas encajadas detrás del plano rojo.

Los objetos se autonomizan como atracción casi puramente visual. En la obra de Martín Mele, esos objetos pierden su determinación como cosas, aunque su mención permanece como vehículo comunicativo. La silla de camping debajo de la tela tensada se percibe aunque finalmente desaparece por completo como tal. Al espectador, al contemplar la obra, los contornos lumínicos se le presentan menos relevantes que la representación de un jarrón de la antigüedad. Se trata de un dorado rectángulo abovedado, un dorado bordeado de azul,

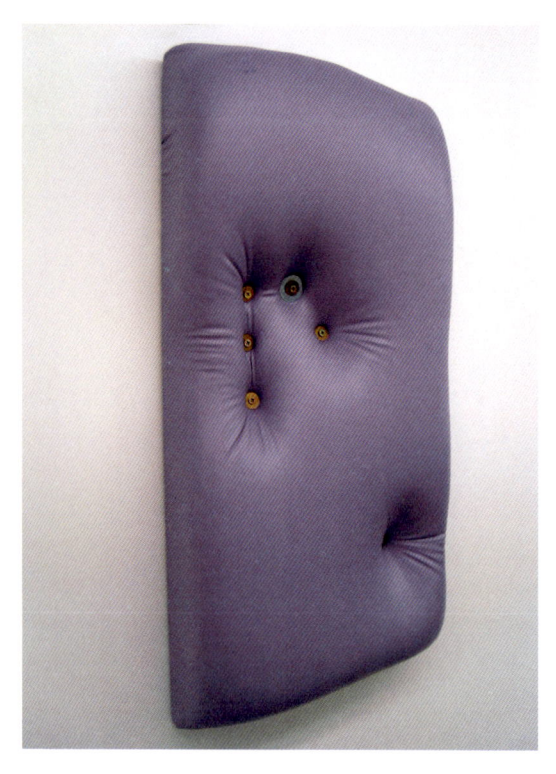

UNTITLED | 2008 | 85 x 50 x 15 cm
UNTITLED | 2008 | 70 x 50 x 15 cm | PRIVATE COLLECTION | MÖNCHENGLADBACH | GERMANY

una superficie brillante, resplandeciente, un rectángulo de noble luminosidad que, debido a su tensión, para ser exactos, ya no es un rectángulo montado sobre la pared sino una presencia casi autónoma visual. En la imagen percibida, la silla se comporta y se manifiesta como el contorno ideal de un jarrón de la antigüedad y esa forma es, a su vez, también portadora de la representación en su conjunto. Son extremidades que se ordenan cual hélices demostrando que pueden – y que demuestran poder – girar alrededor de un centro. Un centro definido por columnas de texto de periódicos que los mantiene unidos. Que las páginas de periódico encubran cosas y que las extremidades sean las patas y el respaldo de la silla, resulta irrelevante, siempre y cuando el espectador no se dé por satisfecho con la simple denominación de lo descubierto. El que se trate de una escultura que lucha por su equilibrio, que se balancea, que parece tambalearse y aún así claramente está en pie, trae a la vista la dinámica impredecible de su estática. Esto también se manifiesta y se percibe cuando las relaciones de los objetos no permanecen en el foco de interés.

Martín Mele juega a ese juego. Él parece ver en lo habitual otra cosa. Muestra lo simple y se refiere a lo complejo. Sin duda, reconoce los valores abstractos en lo concreto.

Untitled | 2009 | *approx. 100 x 110 x 100 cm*

Parece que entiende las formas de las cosas no sólo como una forma de algo cuando va deambulando por las calles recolectando enseres viejos y resíduos, o cuando encuentra su material de trabajo en los mercados de pulga. Porque en los objetos hallados por él siempre surgen valores por encima de lo físico, como, por ejemplo, el valor de la silla, que retrocede detrás de la imágen como cuadro y que – liberada de su función – define el cuadro. Semejándose a Midas, Martín Mele parece ver esculturas y pinturas, donde solo se podría intuir material de trabajo.

When a chair leg becomes a rotor

RAIMUND STECKER

Suitcases upon suitcases, along with plates, vases, mugs, and bowls, piled up on top of one another, like crowns on top. Rolled up carpets and chairs, packaging material and towels, obvious trash and junk bound together with adhesive tape and brought into balance. Cloths that are tightly stretched over walls covering the standard camping chair for lakeside sunbathers are thus present as a relief. Canvases pulled across frames, upholstered with objects that cannot be clearly identified, that strive against the geometrically secure form of painting. Hard foam trunks stick out straight from the wall or in a slightly bent fashion – evoking a grin.

That each chair and every vase, every suitcase, and every walking stick, every roll of carpeting, every candlestick and every bit of hard foam and every thing in general is a sculpture when it is presented to be looked at from an aesthetic aspect, this is something that no longer requires any emphasis. The fact that often a mere plinth, a cobbled together pedestal, or even just the place of presentation is able to expand this function, making a chair not just a seat, a vase more than a container for flowers, a suitcase more than just a travelling utensil, a walking stick more than just an aid in moving, a rolled up carpet not just a form of transportation, a candlestick not just a decorative item to hold a candle, a bit of hard foam not just rubbish, that a special presentation can make normal things into something else is something that by now more or less everyone has come to understand. That such situations can be very frequently found in sites dedicated to art and are still celebrated is no longer surprising, but a bit tiring.

This is different in the work of Martín Mele. He uses all these everyday functional things and arrives at collages and installations, environments and reliefs,

Mosca negra | 2008 | 70 x 50 x 40 cm

Venus | 2009 | 76 x 26 x 26 cm | Private collection | Zürich | Switzerland (top)
Untitled | 2010 | 150 x 45 x 40 cm (right)

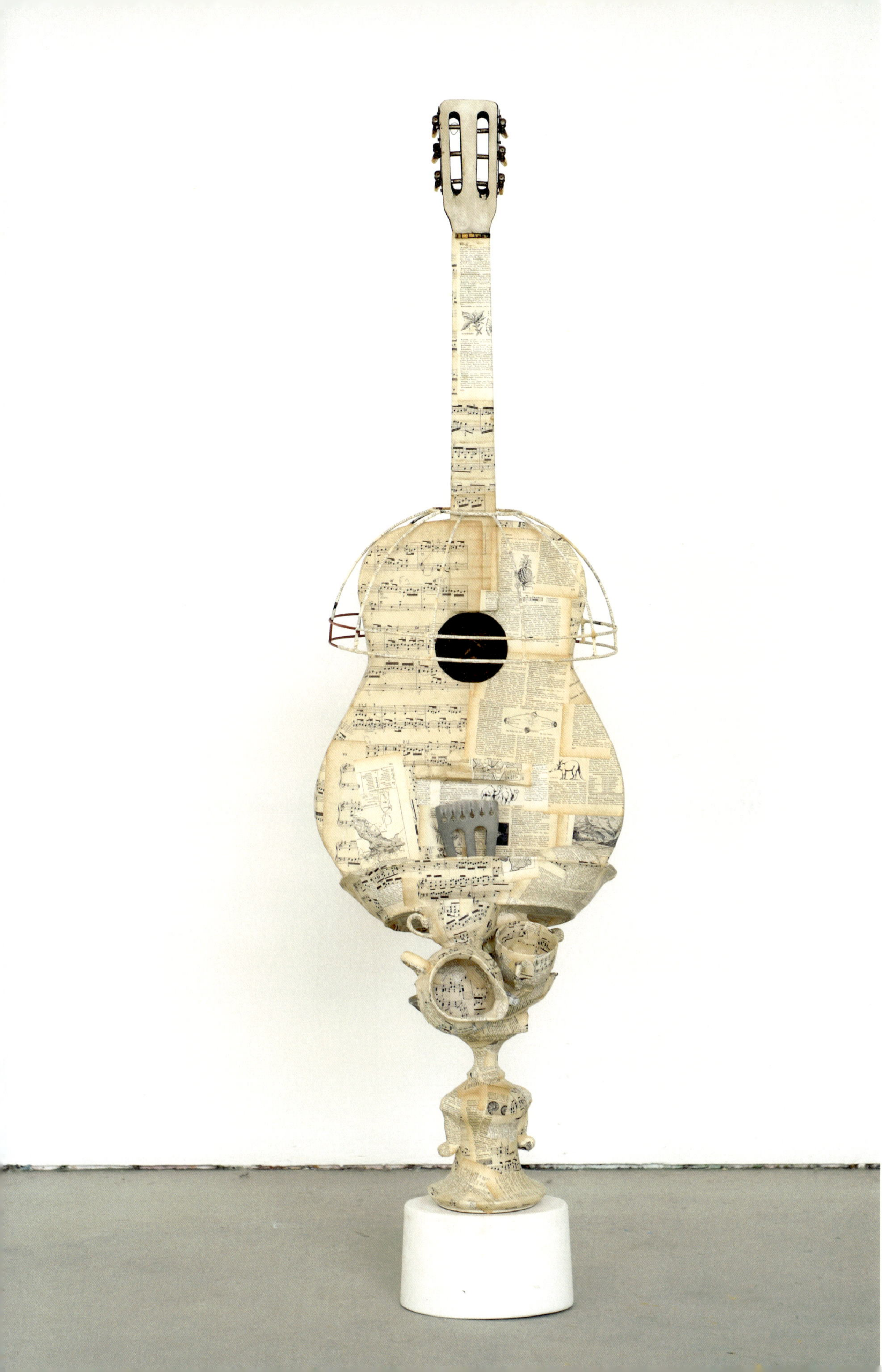

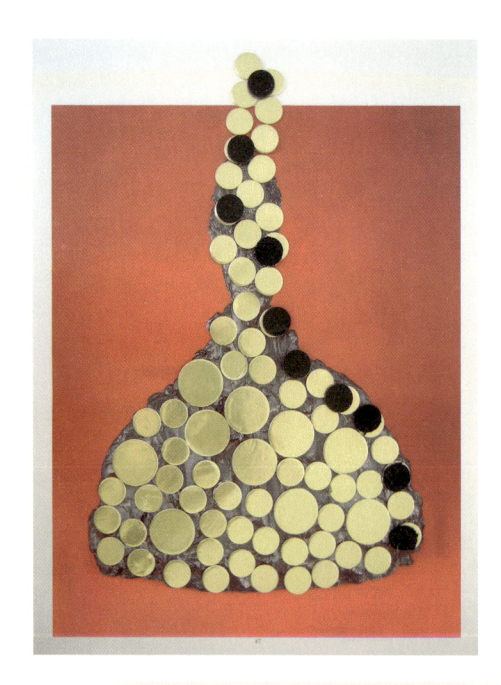

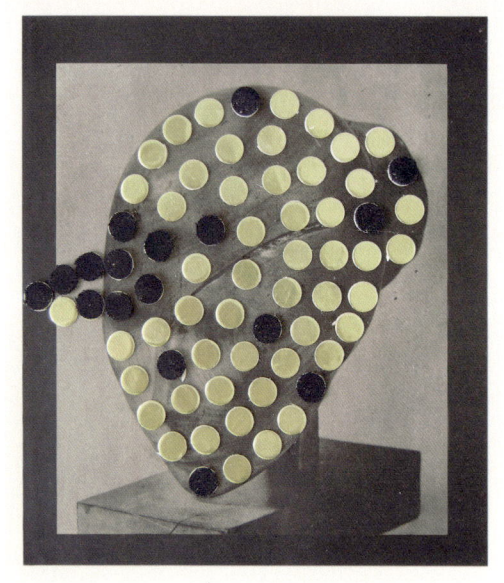

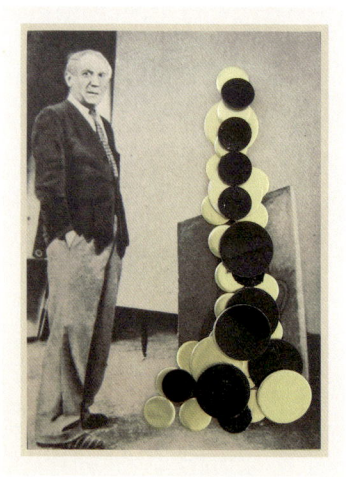

GIACOMETTI | 2010 | 24 x 17,5 cm | COLLAGE (T.L.)
BRANCUSI | 2010 | 23,5 x 17,5 cm | COLLAGE | COLLECTION WETHMAR | DÜSSELDORF | GERMANY (T.R.)
MATARÉ | 2010 | 23,2 x 20,2 cm | COLLAGE | PRIVATE COLLECTION GRAMANN | DÜSSELDORF | GERMANY (B.L.)
PICASSO | 2010 | 16 x 11,5 cm | COLLAGE (B.R.)

Untitled | 2010 | 121 x 30 x 20 cm

2007 | Kunstverein Aichach | Aichach | Germany

situations and works, simply put, to images and sculptures that solely due to their non-functionality can only be one thing: images and sculptures left solely to aesthetic experience.

And what kind of experience do they provide? The red or gold of two wall works, which consist of stretched pieces of cloth and, due to camping chairs, form reliefs, is overwhelming. The chairs, for example, disappear behind the red surface that seems to float in front of the wall, or better, that seems to float through the chairs in front of the wall.

Things becoming autonomous as an almost purely visual attraction seems to be a constant element in the art of Martín Mele. Things in Martín Mele's art lose their thingness, although naming the things used in his works is still a communicative vehicle. The camping chair under the tightly stretched material, however, disappears almost entirely as a camping chair. The outlines that shimmer through prove less important in beholding the work than the scene depicted on an ancient vase. It is a convex golden rectangle, a bit of gold

2007 | Kunstverein Aichach | Aichach | Germany

framed in blue, a shining surface reflecting light, a nobly radiant square that due to its being stretched is actually no longer a square and which mounted on the wall, demands an almost visually autonomous presence. The chair which is to the palpably present image only like a scene applied to the ideal form of an ancient vase, which is ultimately only a support of the representation.

Spinning extremities, like propellers, pretend to rotate around a center. A center holds them together. Columns of text from newspaper pages define this center. That the newspaper pages are glued onto things, and that the extremities are the legs and armrests

2008 | GALERIE MARK MÜLLER | ZÜRICH | SWITZERLAND

of a chair – if one is not satisfied with the simple naming of things that can be recognized – proves to be secondary. That this is a sculpture that struggles to maintain its balance, that seems to reel and yet clearly stands, bringing the unforeseen dynamic in its statics to illustration that also becomes apparent, without realizing the thing-relations – but no, that only becomes apparent when the thing-references do not stand at the center of our interest.

Martín Mele plays this game. He clearly sees in familiar objects what is also different. He shows simple things, and yet means something complex. He recognizes unquestionably abstract values in the concrete. He seems to see the shape of things not solely as thing forms, when he walks through the streets and collects junk, when he uncovers his art material in second-hand shops and flea markets. He recognizes without ambivalence the abstract of shapes and in things. For from the found pieces he uses as the foundation for his sculpture, excessively thingly values emerge, for example, that of the chair which moves behind the image as image, which, stripped of its function, it still helps determine. Like Midas, Martín Mele seems to see sculptures and images where only material is suspected.

Montura | 2009 | 200 x 145 cm

53

Untitled | 2008 | 140 x 100 x 20 cm

55

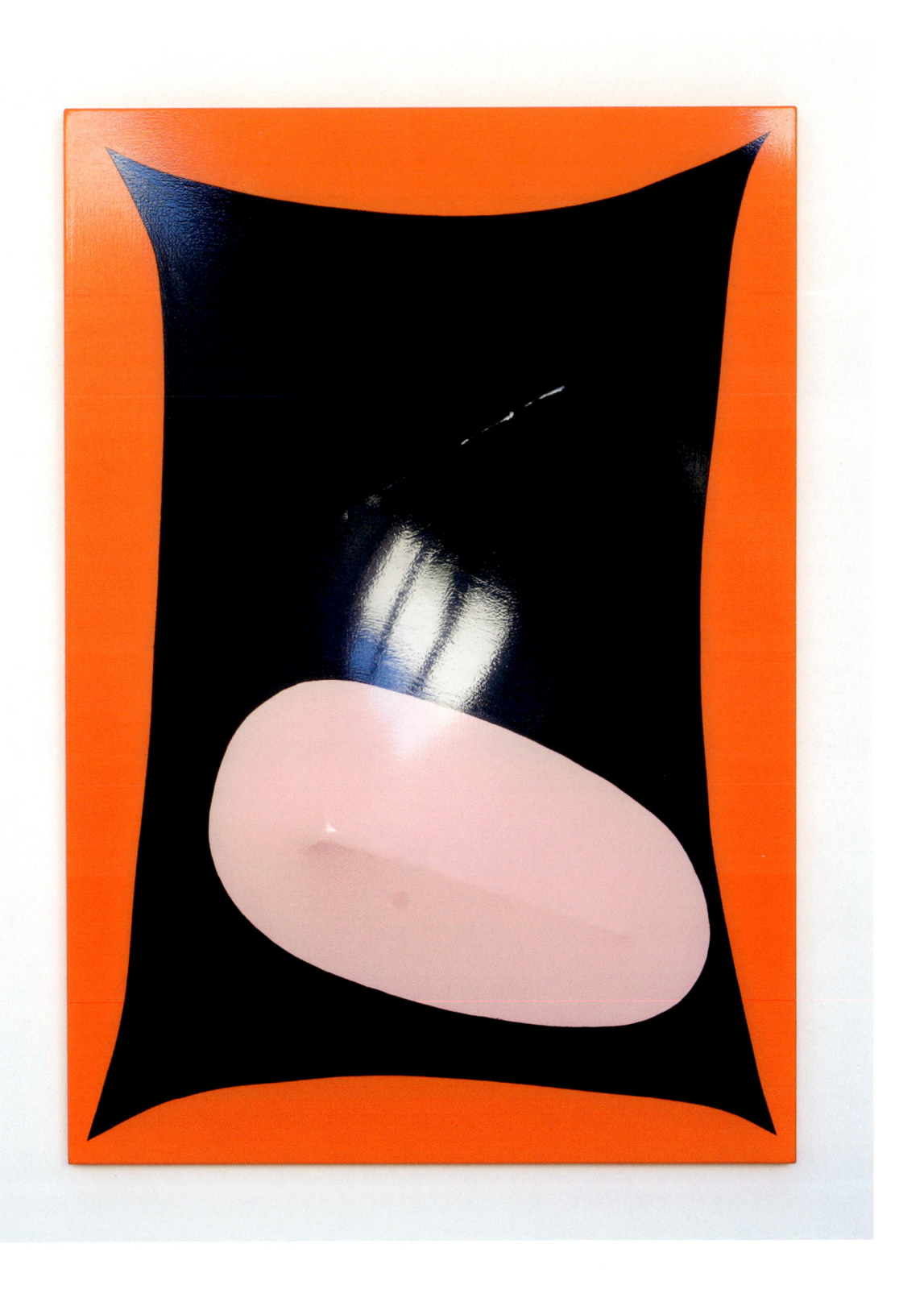

Untitled | 2003 | 250 x 125 x 20 cm

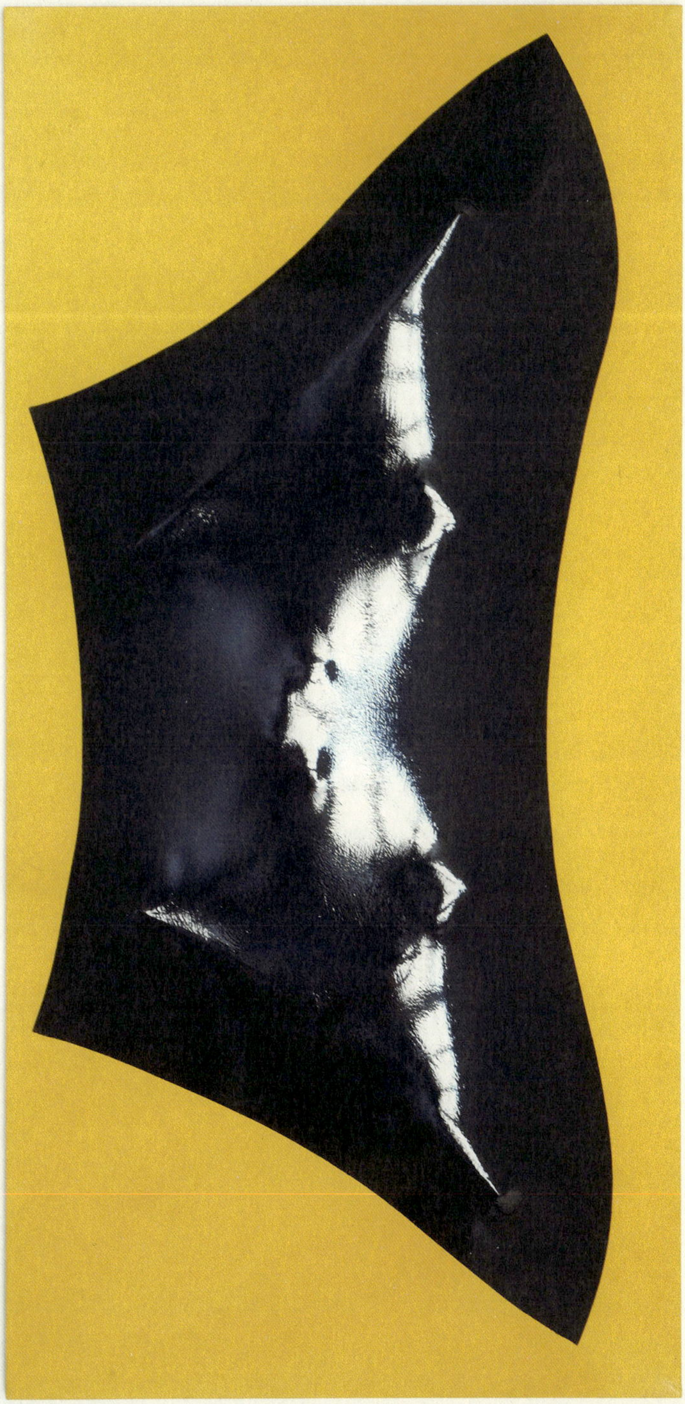

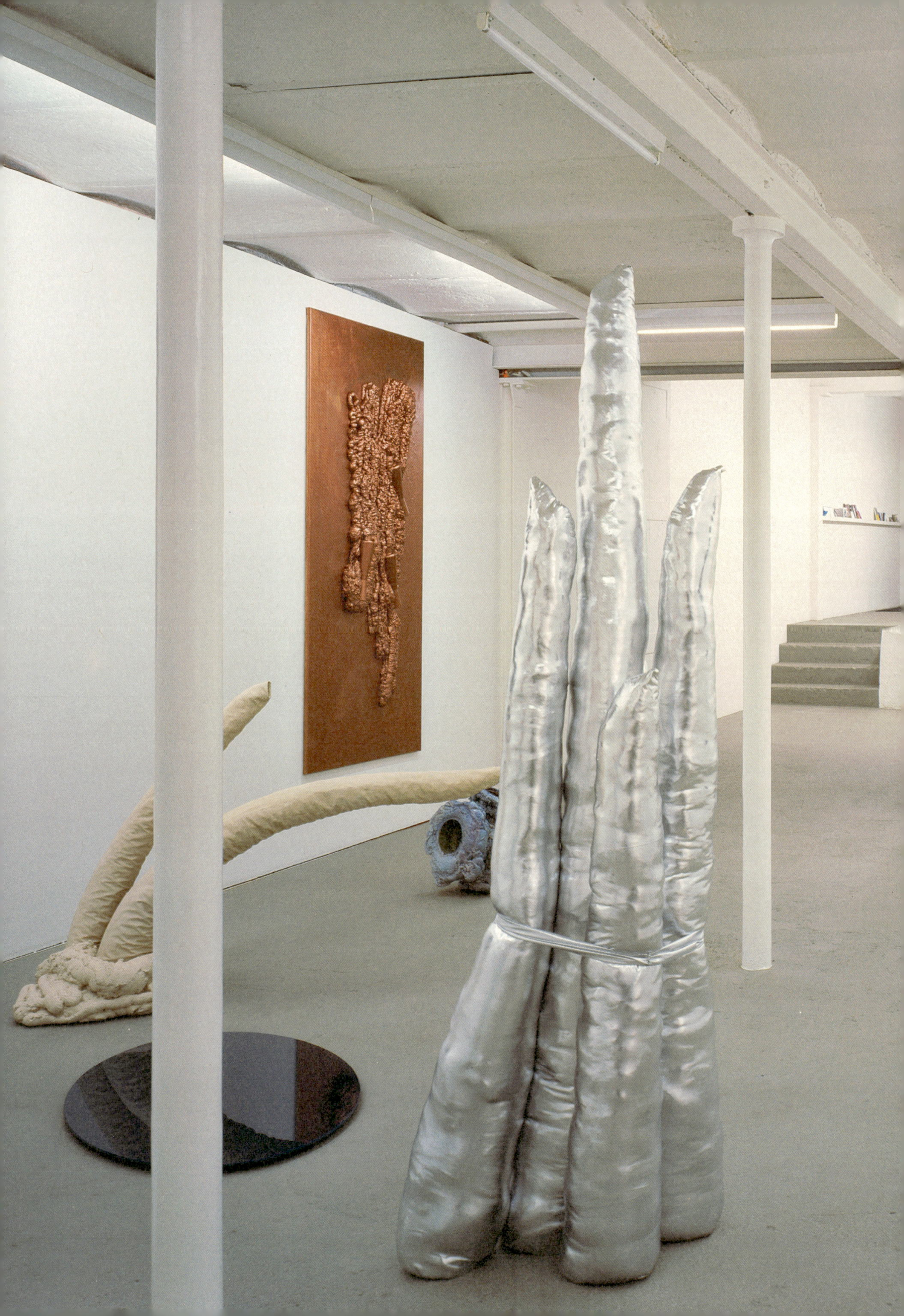

2008 | GALERIE MARK MÜLLER | ZÜRICH | SWITZERLAND

60

2010 | Galerie Cosar EY5 | Düsseldorf | Germany

UNTITLED | 2008 | 45 x 38 x 30 cm (TOP)
UNTITLED | 2008 | 110 x 50 x 50 cm (RIGHT)

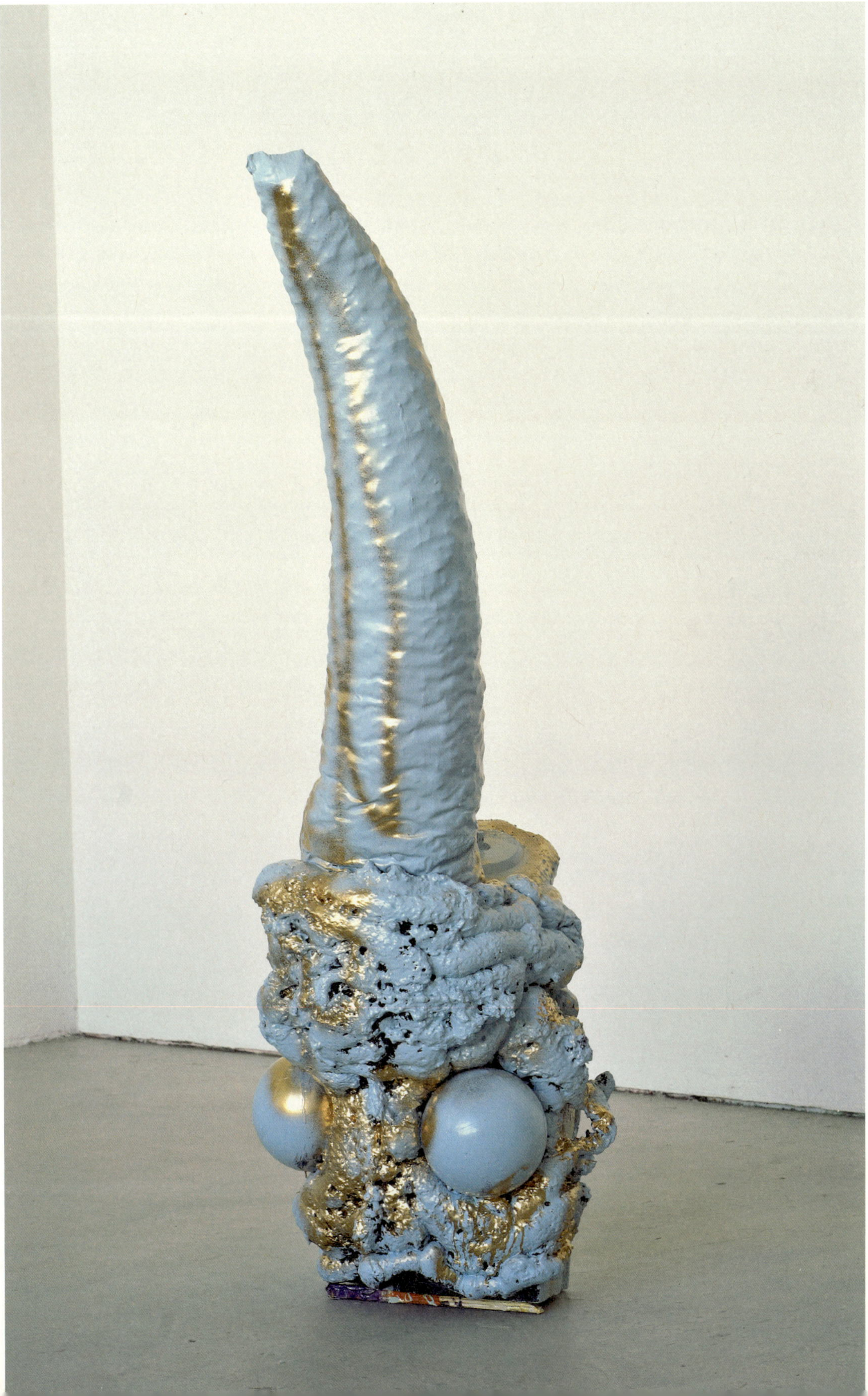

Ready painting | 2008 | 200 x 125 x 20 cm (top)
Untitled | 2010 | 78 x 20 x 20 cm (right)

65

Untitled | 2010 | 110 x 105 x 45 cm (top)
Untitled | 2010 | 135 x 35 x 35 cm (right)

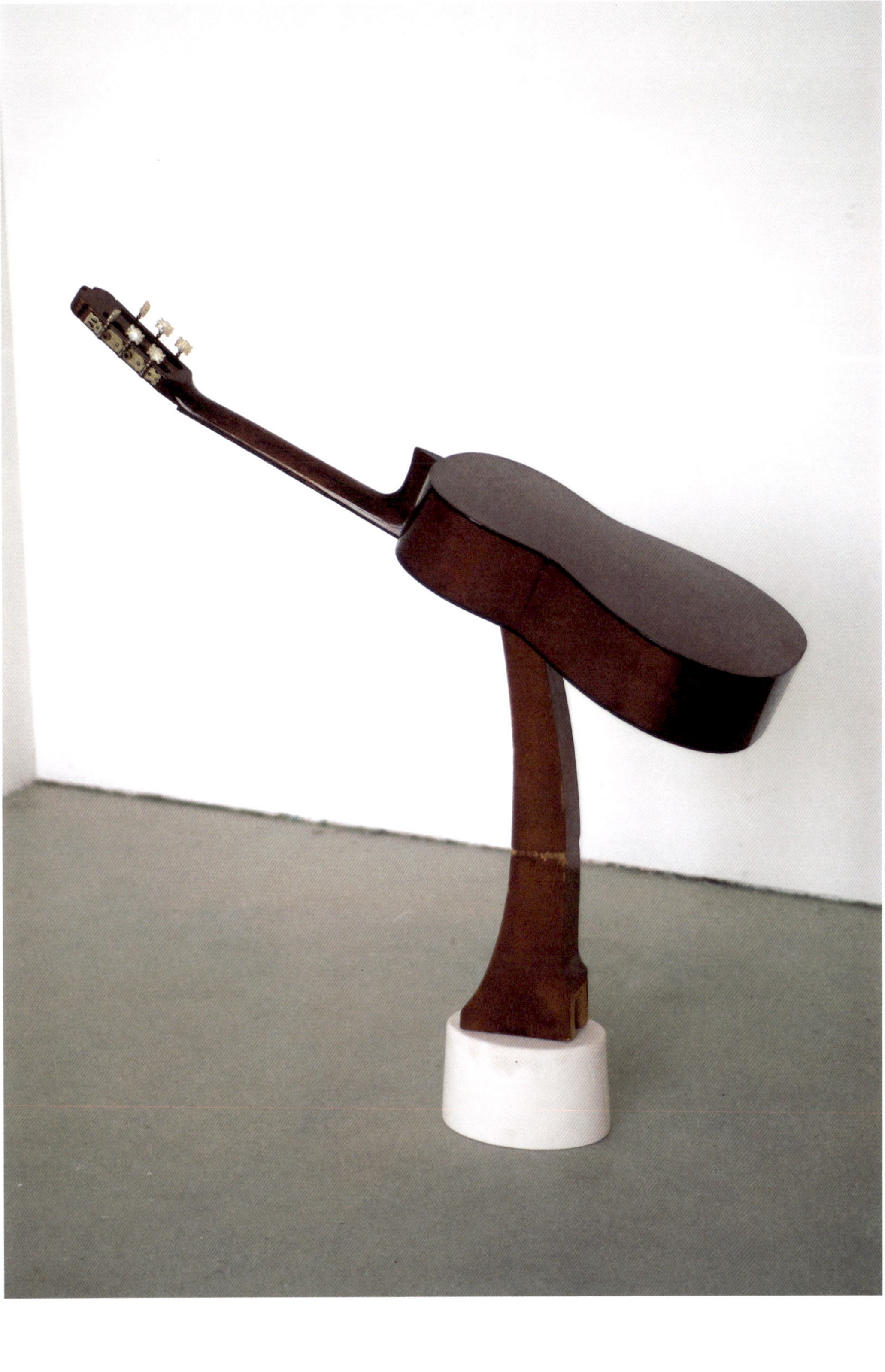

Untitled | 2010 | 80 x 90 x 50 cm

69

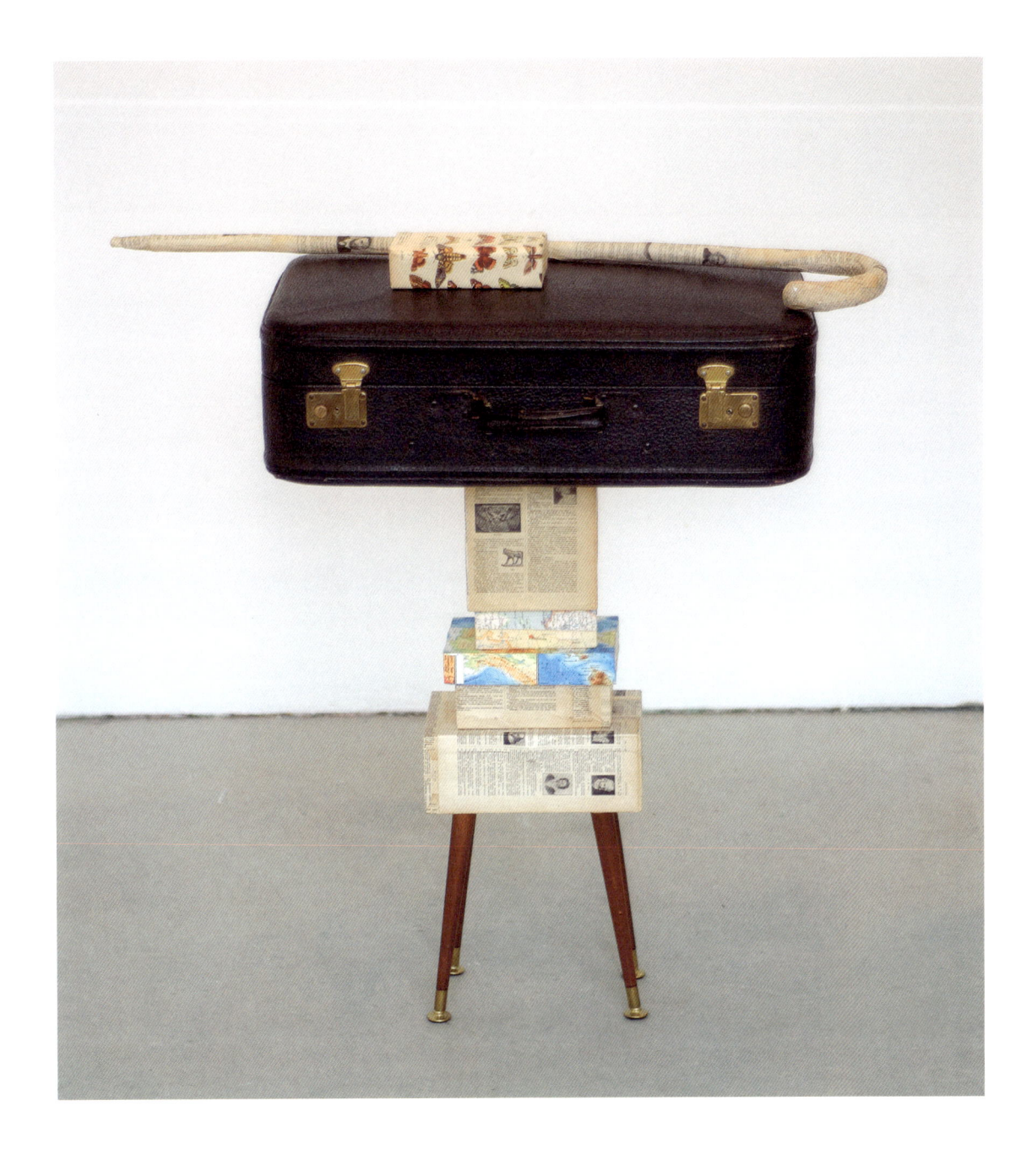

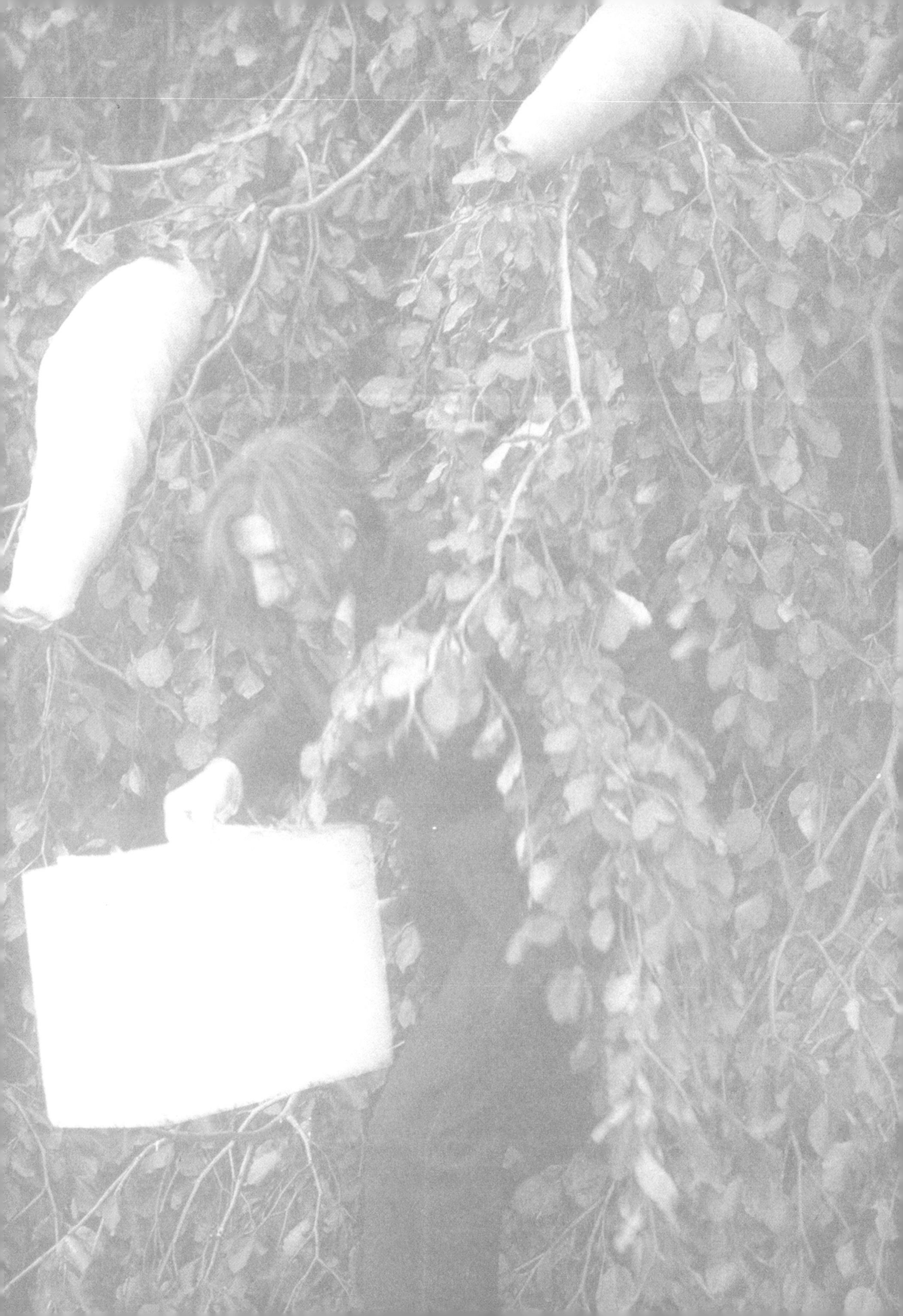

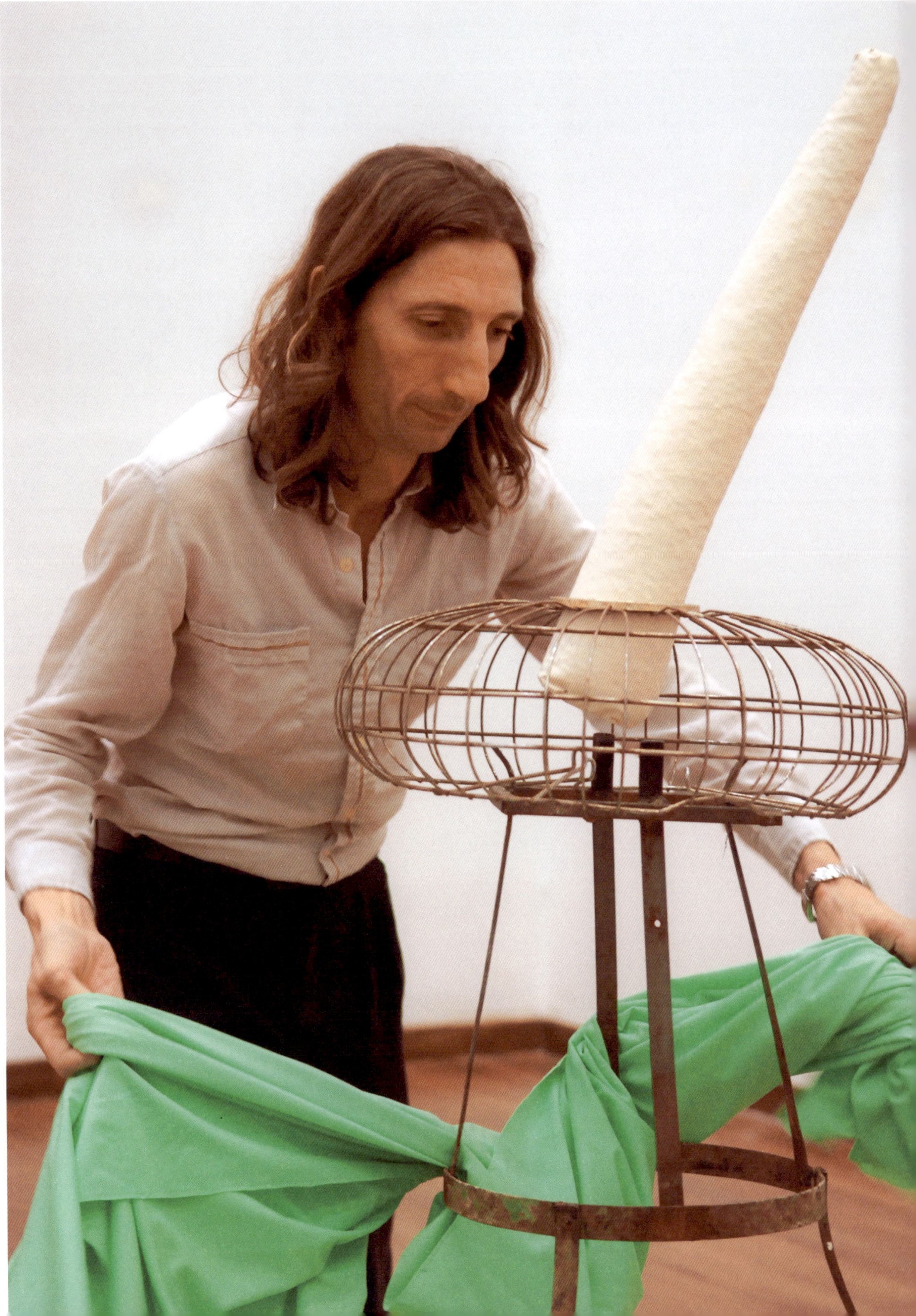

Das Archiv im Wurm

ANDRÉS DUPRAT

Der Künstler, der in Argentinien und Deutschland lebt und arbeitet, unternimmt eine kreative Reise quer durch zwei Kontinente, acht Städte, und über mehrere tausend Kilometer. Der Plan: eine radikale Erfahrung, die sich die an den jeweiligen Schauplätzen vorgefundenen Objekte zunutze macht.

„In die Mitte des Mülls stellt Mele einen leichten Klappstuhl, der als vorläufige Basis der Arbeit gilt. Mit einer Auswahl farbiger Klebstreifen befestigt er verschiedene Objekte auf und an dem Stuhl. Dazu gehören frisch gefüllte, kleinere Plastiktüten und Gegenstände wie alte Schrubber, Eimer, Stoff, Rahmen, Schachteln, und Dosen. Zunächst sind Meles Bewegungen gezielt und werden nur hin und wieder unterbrochen, um sich selbst im Video beim Arbeiten zuzusehen. Während die Form jedoch wächst, werden seine Bewegungen zunehmend schneller, hektischer, sogar aggressiv. Er greift einen Stuhl und versucht, ihn in der Mitte durchzusägen, was ihm aber nicht gelingt. Nach einem kurzen Kampf zerbricht er den Stuhl gewaltsam am Boden und befestigt die einzelnen Teile an der wachsenden Arbeit. Weitere Objekte werden mit Klebstreifen hinzugefügt und abgesichert, indem er sie zeitweilig rennend umkreist, wobei er kleinere Gegenstände aus dem Weg tritt. Zuletzt zieht er das Gebilde von der Bühne, dreht es um, stellt es auf eine kleine Holzkiste und befestigt das Ganze mit weiteren Objekten und Klebstreifen. Nach ungefähr fünfzehn Minuten anstrengender und konzentrierter Arbeit ist die neue Form nun zusammenhängend komplett. Mele zieht noch eine letzte Runde mit Klebstreifen, harpuniert das Ganze mit einem Gehstock und hängt als Abschluss einen Keilrahmen oben drauf. Kurz betrachtet er die fertig gestellte Arbeit und wendet sich wieder seinen Gästen zu."

[Exzerpt aus einem Text von Emi Winter und Steffen Böddeker über die Performance von Martín Mele im Museum für zeitgenössische Kunst von Oaxaca, Mexiko 2007. (Museo de Arte Contemporáneo de Oaxaca)]

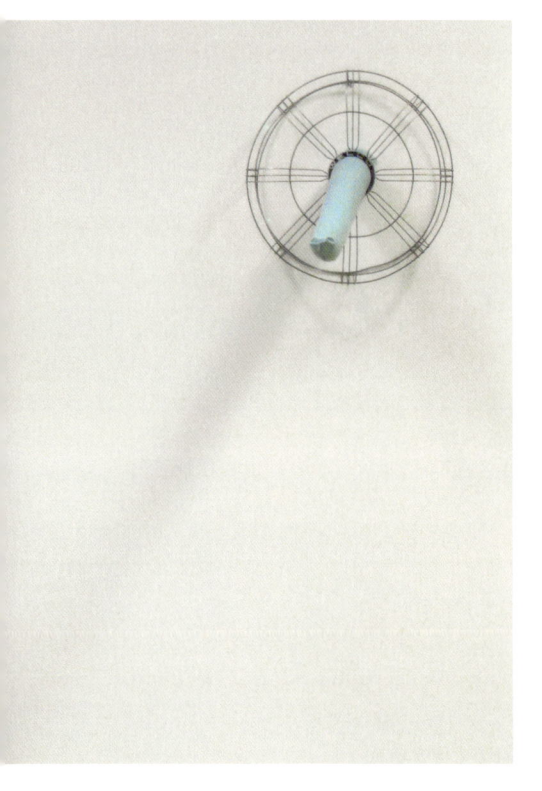

Das Vorhaben des argentinischen Künstlers Martín Mele (1960 in Buenos Aires geboren) gründet im Kern auf der Idee der Reise als Erfahrung. Das Projekt sprengt das Format einer Ausstellung oder Performance und beinhaltet weit mehr als das, was man gemeinhin als Wanderausstellung bezeichnet. Es handelt sich vielmehr um eine radikale Erfahrung, die bewusst das Risiko sucht und die Entstehung des Werkes selbst beeinflusst. Die Aktion operiert direkt am Herz und Nervensystem der Kunstproduktion an sich.

Mit dem *Archiv im Wurm* begibt sich Mele auf eine Reise – körperlich wie geistig –, die zwei Kontinente, acht Städte und eine Wegstrecke von Tausenden von Kilometern umfasst. Auf diese Weise verwandeln sich die Werke in Aktionen (Handlung), die durch die Auswirkungen der ständigen Standortwechsel beeinflusst werden. Die Kunst entsteht an den Kreuzwegen der Erfahrung, in der Zwiesprache mit dem jeweiligen Raum sowie mit seinen Wechselfällen und der Eigenschaft der Objekte.

Das Projekt, vom argentinischen Kulturministerium und der Kunststiftung NRW unterstützt, ist auf zwei Etappen ausgelegt. Ebenso definiert sich die Arbeitsmethode durch zwei Grundsatzentscheidungen: den Ausgangspunkt und die geplante Reiseroute. Auf

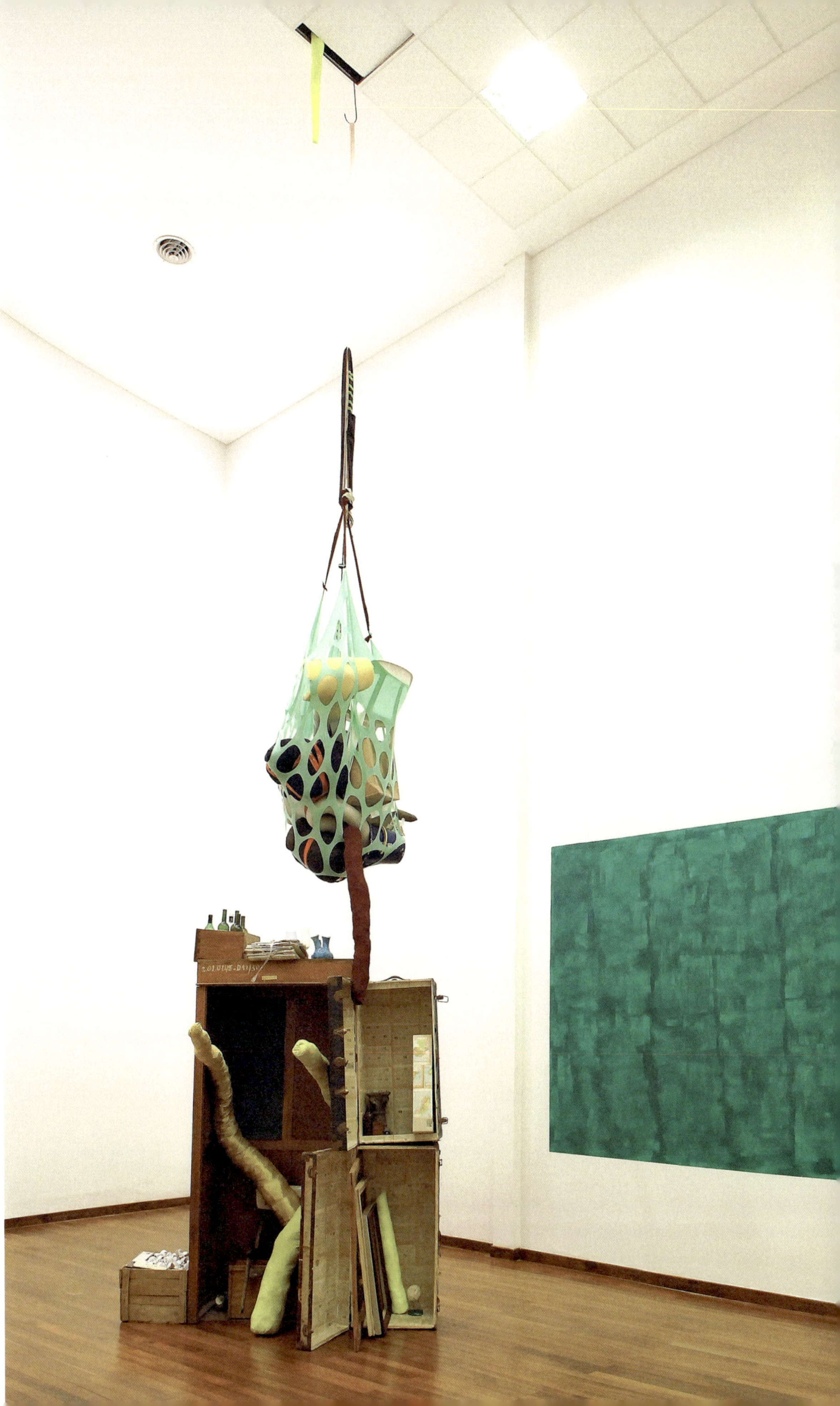

der ersten Etappe unternimmt Mele eine vier Wochen dauernde veritable *tour de force durch* Argentinien: Reisen, Sammeln, Herstellen und Vorführen der Arbeiten in den vier Städten Salta, Rosario, Neuquén und Ushuaia. Mele hat das Unternehmen als ästhetisches Experimentierfeld angelegt, in dem die Empirie Methode ist – und das Ergebnis daher unvorhersehbar.

Der Künstler sammelt, fügt zusammen, arrangiert, korrigiert, zerschlägt, nimmt auseinander. Seine Werkzeuge: Blick, Reflexion, Sachkenntnis, Instinkt, Überzeugung, Versuch und – eben auch – Irrtum, Fehltritt, Zweifel und Zufall. Alles wird sichtbar, alles offenbart sich, es entsteht ein Hier und Jetzt der Erfahrung der Dinge als solche. Und doch tritt, ist das Werk einmal installiert, auch sofort ein gewisser Verlust an Lebendigkeit zutage und bleibt zurück wie eine Spur, ein Indiz, ein stummer Zeuge.

Mele gibt die Entstehung der Ideen, der Fundstücke und ihrer Derivate dem öffentlichen Blick Preis. Er verwandelt den Ausstellungsraum in ein offenes Atelier und unterläuft so etablierte gesellschaftliche Gepflogenheiten: die Idee von der Präsentation des vollendeten Werkes, die Vernissagen, die Rollen, die dem Publikum und dem Künstler zugedacht sind, das Konzept von Betrachter und Spektakel, die Sinnhaftigkeit der einsamen Arbeit des Künstlers. Er stellt überraschende Bezüge her und verleiht dergestalt seinem Werk eine außergewöhnliche gesellschaftliche Dimension. Die Objekte erwachen zum Leben, indem sie Beziehungen knüpfen: Sie setzen gesellschaftliche und stoffliche Beziehungen auf der Bühne des Lebens in Szene. Sie sind die verdichtete Erfahrung gesellschaftlicher und stofflicher Gegebenheiten.

Indem Meles Aktion sich aus dem Aufeinandertreffen von Schauplatz und künstlerischer Erfahrung, persönlichen Wahrnehmungen und Vorstellungen entfaltet, entsteht das Werk „in" und „aus" diesem einzigartigen und besonderen Kontakt. Innerhalb eines Monats entwickelt und zeigt Mele im Februar seine Arbeiten im Museo de Bellas Artes de Salta, im Museo de Arte Contemporáneo de Rosario, im Museo Nacional de Bellas Artes de Neuquén und im März 2010 im Museo Marítimo de Ushuaia. Sobald die Aktion des Künstlers in allen Museen stattgefunden hat, bleiben die vier Museen für das Publikum simultan geöffnet und können im April besucht werden.

Die zweite Etappe findet nach ähnlichen Gesichtspunkten in der zweiten Jahreshälfte 2010 in Europa statt und führt über Institutionen in Frankfurt, Biel, Berlin und Neuss. Den Zyklus beschließt die Herausgabe dieses Buches, in dem das gesamte Projekt zusammengetragen und dokumentiert ist.

Das Wechselspiel zwischen den beiden Kontinenten eröffnet verschiedenartige Möglichkeiten und erzeugt voneinander abweichende Ergebnisse, die zu tun haben mit der jeweils besonderen Beziehung zwischen Stadt, Kontext, Eigenheiten des Ausstellungsraumes und – zufälligen – Umständen, denen sich der Künstler in jedem Moment seiner Irrfahrt gegenübersieht. Mele – unbußfertiger Pilger, in Holland aufgewachsener Argentinier, und während der letzten zwanzig Jahre Pendler zwischen Wohnsitzen in Deutschland und Argentinien – verkörpert die Sehweise, die durch das viele Hin- und Herreisen zwischen Europa und Amerika geprägt ist – ein Topos der argentinischen Kultur. Seine Reise ist in diesem Fall jedoch eine besondere, eine Art Wiedergutmachung, eingefärbt mit einer persönlichen

77

SALTA MUSEO DE BELLAS ARTES

Note, die Borges´ Ausspruch „Wir Argentinier sind Europäer im Exil" umkehrt oder zumindest hinterfragt.

Die Reise gerät zum Dreh- und Angelpunkt der Ausstellung: Für den Künstler und seine zahlreichen Ortswechsel ebenso wie für die Objekte, die er sammelt, auswählt, transferiert, aus dem Zusammenhang reißt, manipuliert und verfälscht, um seine Werke zu schaffen, und damit gewissermaßen den eigenen Ursprung, den Weg und das Ziel ständig ändert. Das Material von Meles Arbeiten sind Fundstücke, die am Wegrand liegen. Und *Das Archiv im Wurm* erzählt von dem, was bleibt, wenn die Zeit den Berg der Erfahrung abgetragen hat: Der Wurm hat das Archiv verschlungen. Mele schlägt uns vor, diesem Befund ohne Umschweife ins Auge zu blicken. Das Archiv ist seine persönliche Erinnerung.

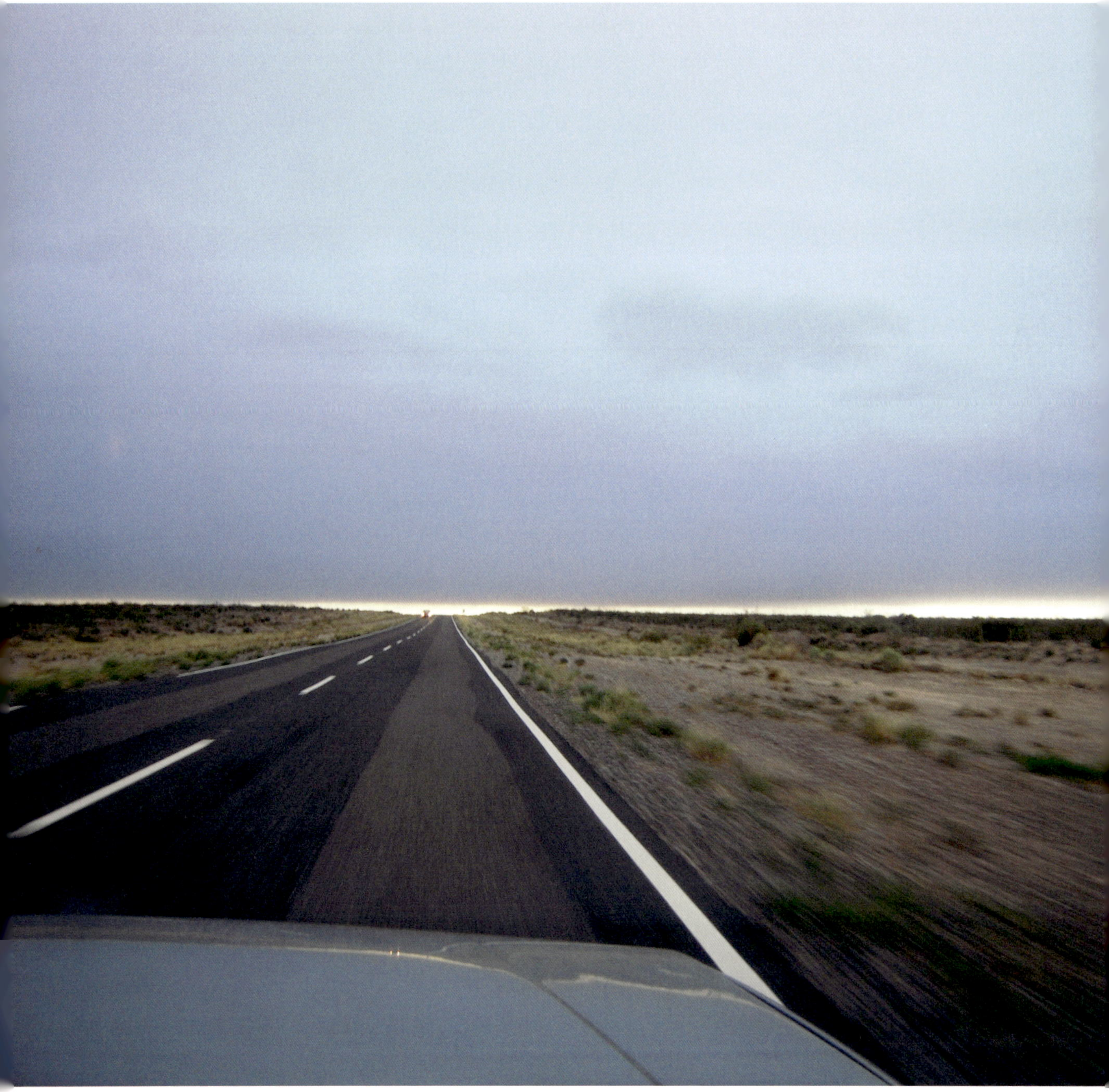

El Archivo en la Polilla

Andrés Duprat

El artista, que vive y trabaja entre Argentina y Alemania, emprende un viaje creativo a través de dos continentes, ocho ciudades y miles de kilómetros. La propuesta: una experiencia radical que se vale de los objetos de cada lugar.

"Mele colocó una silla, que serviría de soporte inicial para la escultura, sobre el montón de basura. Con su arsenal de cintas adhesivas de colores, comenzó a atarle todo tipo de objetos: primero, bolsas chicas rellenas y luego, trapeadores viejos, cubetas, muebles, telas, marcos rotos, cajas y latas. Al principio, sus acciones fueron deliberadas, y de vez en cuando pausaba para observar su imagen proyectada en la pared, pero conforme la masa fue creciendo, sus movimientos se volvieron rápidos, frenéticos y hasta violentos. Finalmente, bajó la pieza de la plataforma, la arrastró, la volteó sobre una caja de madera, le incorporó más objetos y la volvió a amarrar para estabilizarla. De la silla que, originalmente, había servido de soporte, sólo se veían las patas que salían por un lado. Después de quince minutos de intenso trabajo físico y concentración, la forma extraña se volvió coherente. Mele le dio una última vuelta con cinta, ató un bastón en su centro y colgó un bastidor en el palo de un trapeador. Consideró la obra brevemente, tomó su saco y se retiró".

[Fragmento del texto de Emi Winter y Steffen Böddeker acerca de la acción de Martín Mele en el Museo de Arte Contemporáneo de Oaxaca, México, en 2007]

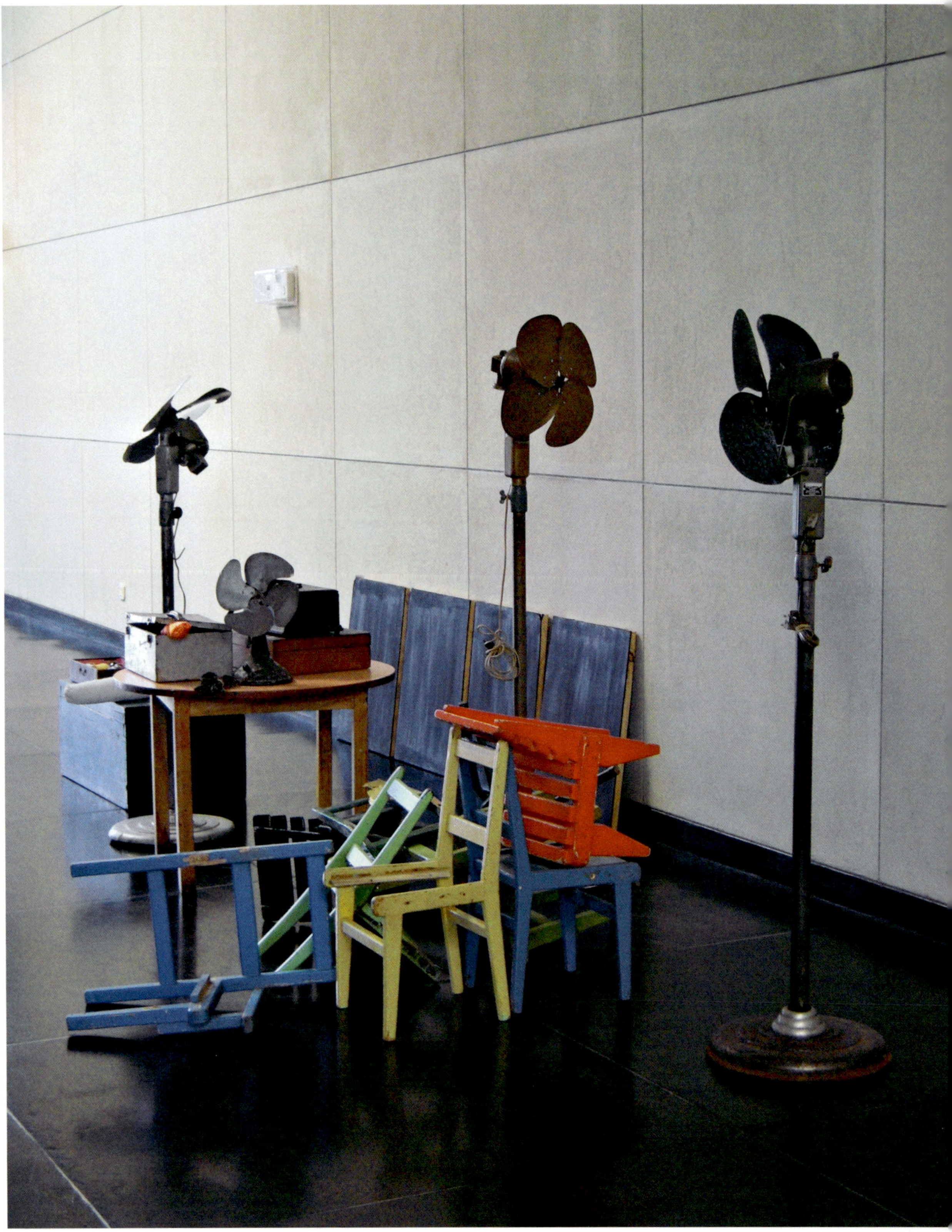

La propuesta del artista argentino Martín Mele (Buenos Aires, 1960) se funda en un concepto esencial: el viaje como experiencia. El proyecto excede el formato de exposición y el de performance, e incluso va más allá de lo que corrientemente llamamos muestra itinerante. Se trata de una experiencia radical, no exenta de riesgos, capaz de influir en forma determinante en la propia génesis de la obra. Una acción que opera directamente en el sistema de creación y producción de la obra de arte.

Con El Archivo en la Polilla, Mele se embarca en un viaje – tanto físico como mental –, que involucra dos continentes, ocho ciudades y miles de kilómetros de travesía. De esta manera, las obras se transforman en acciones, influidas por las implicancias de sus continuos traslados. Y el arte se genera en los cruces entre la experiencia, el diálogo con cada ámbito de su peripecia y la cualidad de los objetos.

Pensado en dos etapas, este proyecto, que cuenta con el apoyo de la Secretaría de Cultura de la Nación y de la Kunststiftung NRW, de Alemania, propone una mecánica de trabajo que se define a partir de dos decisiones determinantes: un punto de partida y un itinerario geográfico establecido. En la primera etapa, Mele emprende un verdadero *tour de force* de un mes de duración, viajando, acopiando, creando y presentando sus trabajos en cuatro ciudades del país: Salta, Rosario, Neuquén y Ushuaia. Plantea este ejercicio como un campo de experimentación estética en el que el empirismo es el método, y, por ende, el resultado es impredecible.

El artista recoge, ensambla, coloca, corrige, rompe, desarma: sus instrumentos son, entonces, su mirada, sus reflexiones, su pericia, su instinto, sus convicciones, sus pruebas y, por supuesto, sus errores, tropiezos, dudas y accidentes. Todo se ve, todo se muestra, hay un hacerse presente de la experiencia en las cosas. Y, una vez plasmada la obra, también se vuelve patente cierta pérdida de lo vivido, que resta como vestigio, como indicio, como testigo mudo.

De esta manera, Mele expone la génesis de sus ideas, sus hallazgos y sus derivas ante la mirada pública. Transforma la sala de exposición en taller abierto, tergiversando así prácticas sociales establecidas, como la idea de exposición de la obra concluida, las inauguraciones, los roles del público y de los creadores, los conceptos de espectador y espectáculo, el sentido del trabajo solitario del artista, en tanto confiere a su obra una inusitada dimensión relacional y social. Sus objetos viven porque cuajan vínculos: ponen en acto los vínculos sociales y materiales en el mundo de la vida. Son experiencia condensada, hechos sociales hechos objeto.

Al desplegar su acción en el encuentro del espacio expositivo con su experiencia artística y sus percepciones e imaginarios personales, la obra se genera "en" y "a partir de" ese contacto único y particular. En el lapso de un mes, durante febrero, Mele desarrolló y presentó sus trabajos en el Museo de Bellas Artes de Salta, el Museo de Arte Contemporáneo de Rosario, el Museo Nacional de Bellas Artes de Neuquén y, en marzo 2010, lo hizo en el Museo Marítimo de Ushuaia. Una vez concluida la acción del artista en cada museo, las cuatro muestras permanecen abiertas al público en forma simultánea, y pueden visitarse durante abril.

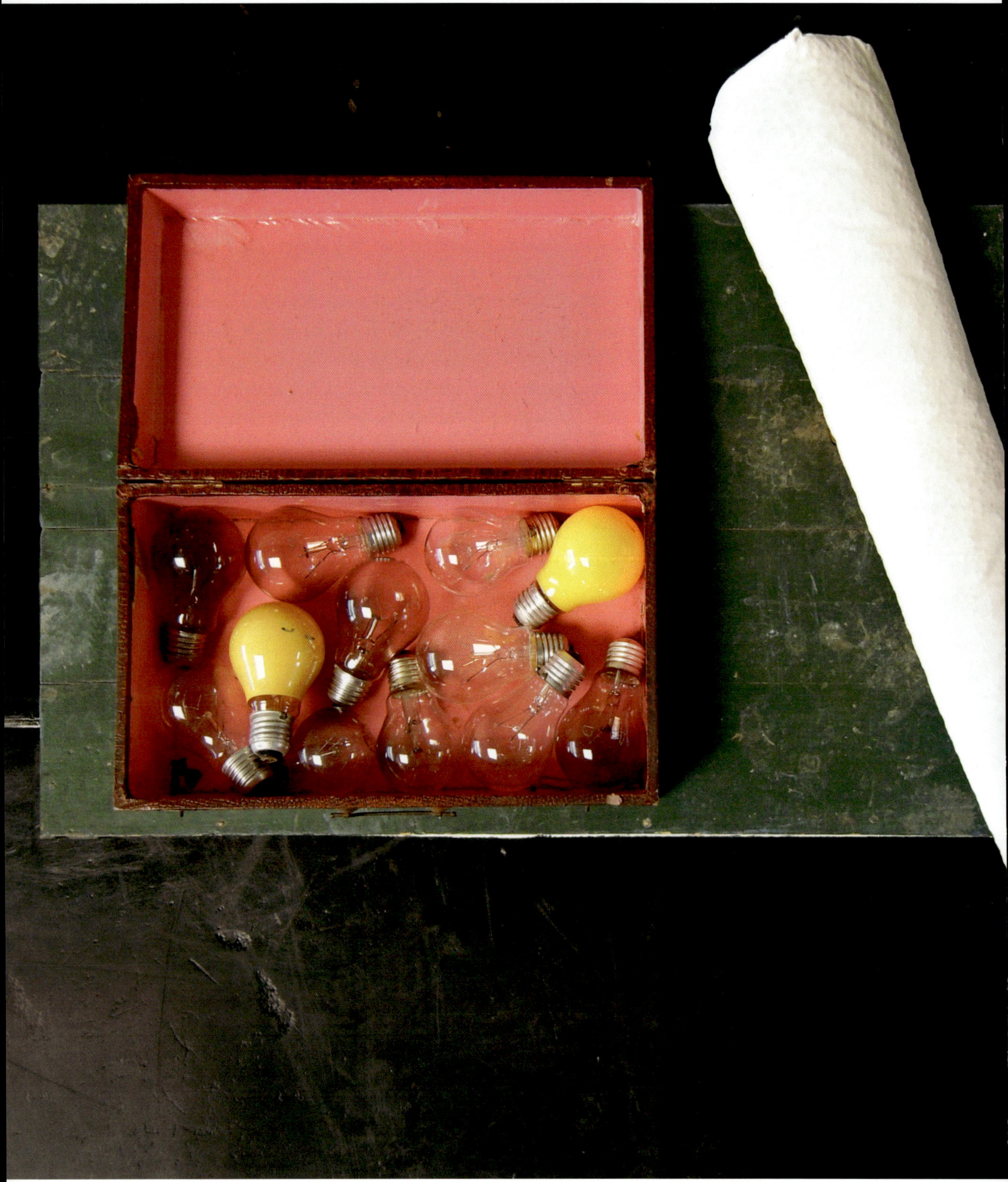

La segunda etapa, de características similares, se llevó a cabo en el segundo semestre de 2010 en Europa, e involucró instituciones de Francfort, Biel, Berlín y Neuss. Al final del ciclo, se editó este libro que compila y documenta todo el proyecto.

La peripecia entre ambos continentes brinda diferentes posibilidades y genera resultados diversos que tienen que ver con la relación específica entre la ciudad, el contexto, las características del espacio expositivo y las circunstancias – aleatorias – a las que el artista se enfrenta en cada momento de su errancia. Viajero impenitente, argentino criado en Holanda, y, en los últimos veinte años, residente alternativo entre Alemania y Argentina, Mele encarna la mirada tramada de múltiples viajes entre Europa y América, un tópico de la cultura argentina. Es el suyo, entonces, un viaje peculiar con algo de reparación, teñido de una dimensión personal que invierte o, al menos, interroga el dictum borgiano "los argentinos somos europeos en el exilio".

El viaje se transforma en eje de la exposición tanto para el artista y sus múltiples traslados, como para los objetos que este recolecta, selecciona, traslada, descontextualiza, manipula y tergiversa para crear sus obras, modificando, de alguna manera, su origen, su destino y su trayectoria. Los materiales plásticos son los hallazgos que el camino le depara. Y *El Archivo en la Polilla* habla de lo que queda cuando el tiempo ha arrasado la experiencia: la polilla ha devorado el archivo. Mele propone ver, en acto, ese resultado. El archivo es su memoria personal.

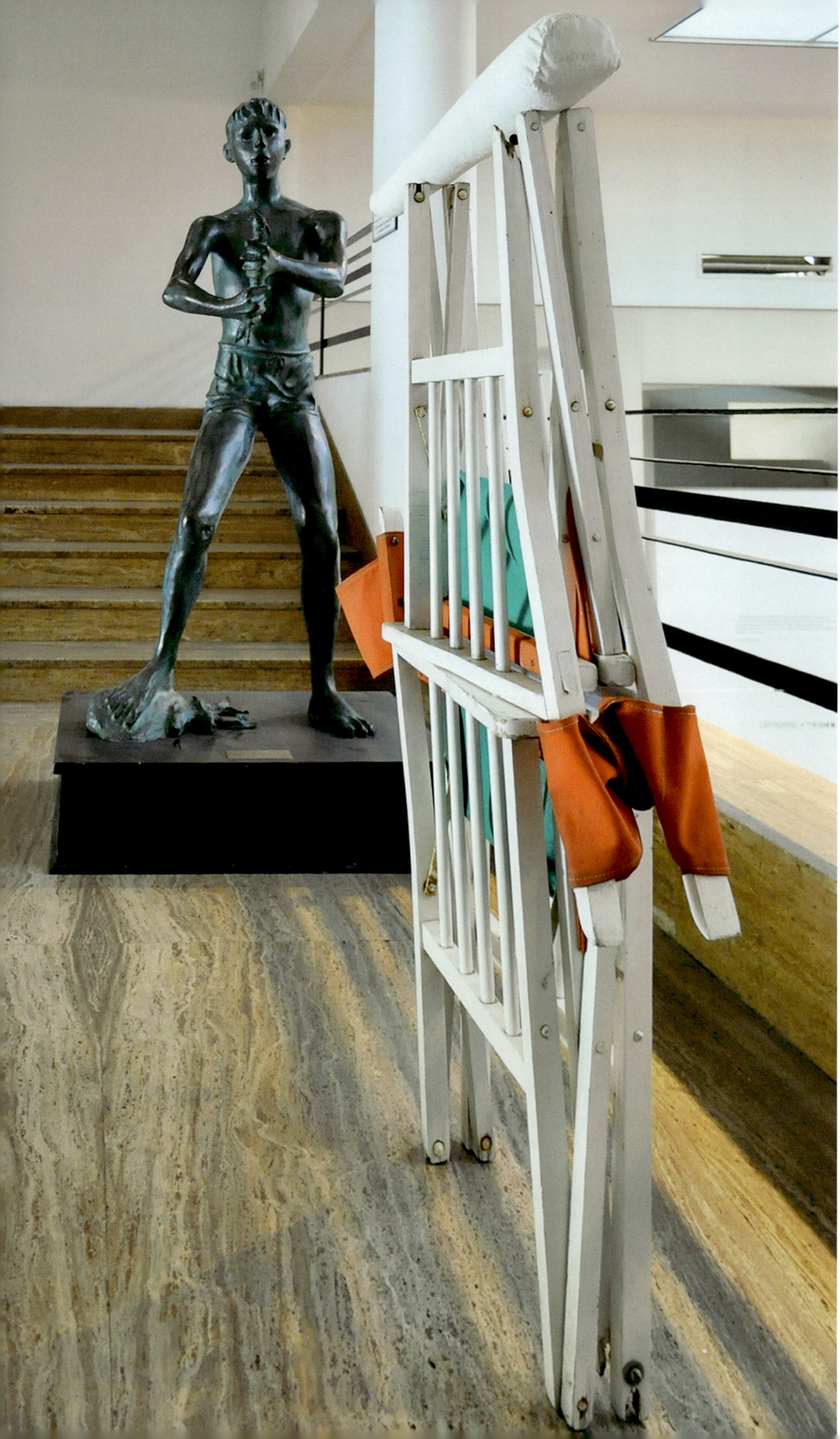

87 Rosario Museo Castagnino

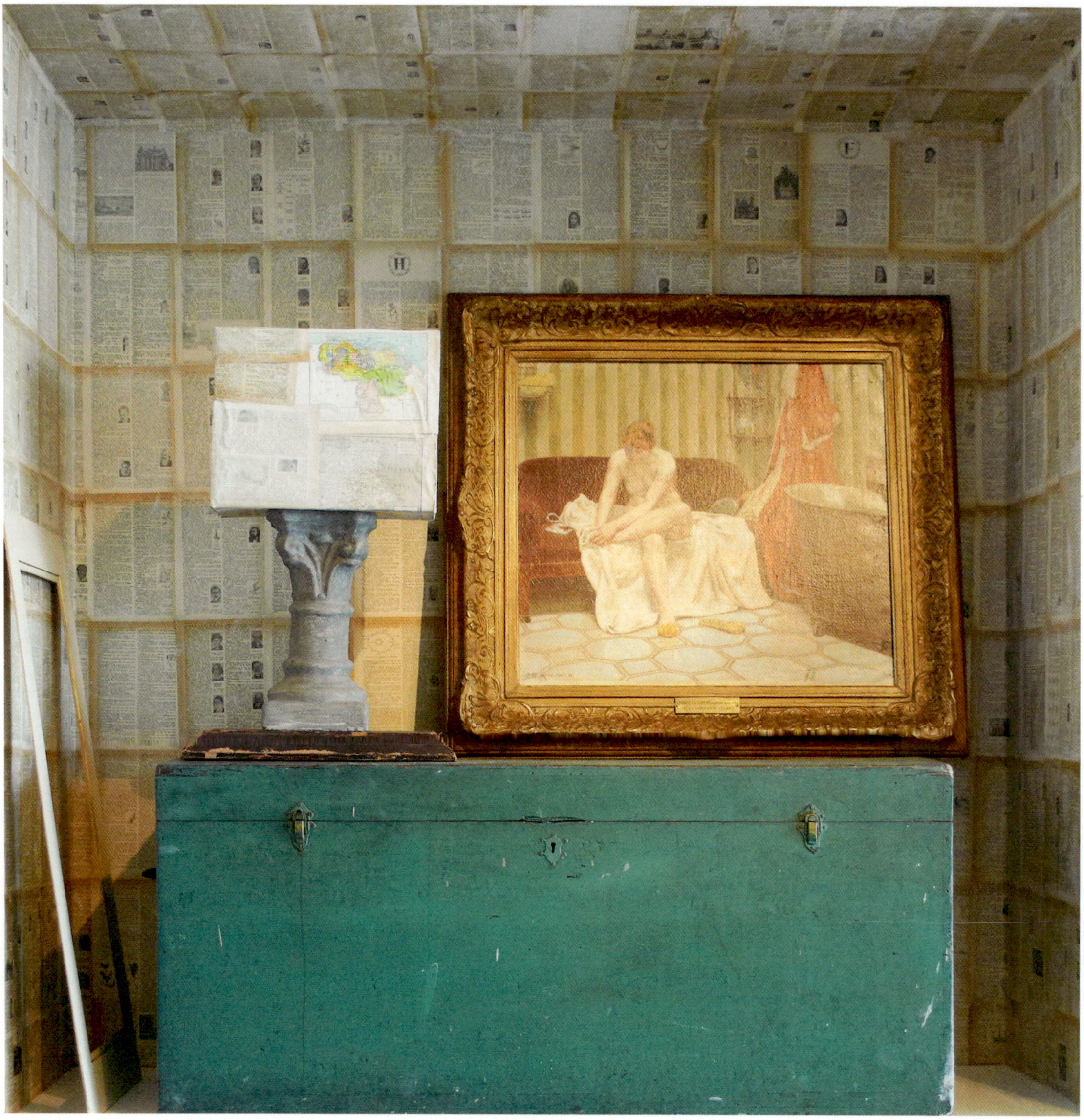

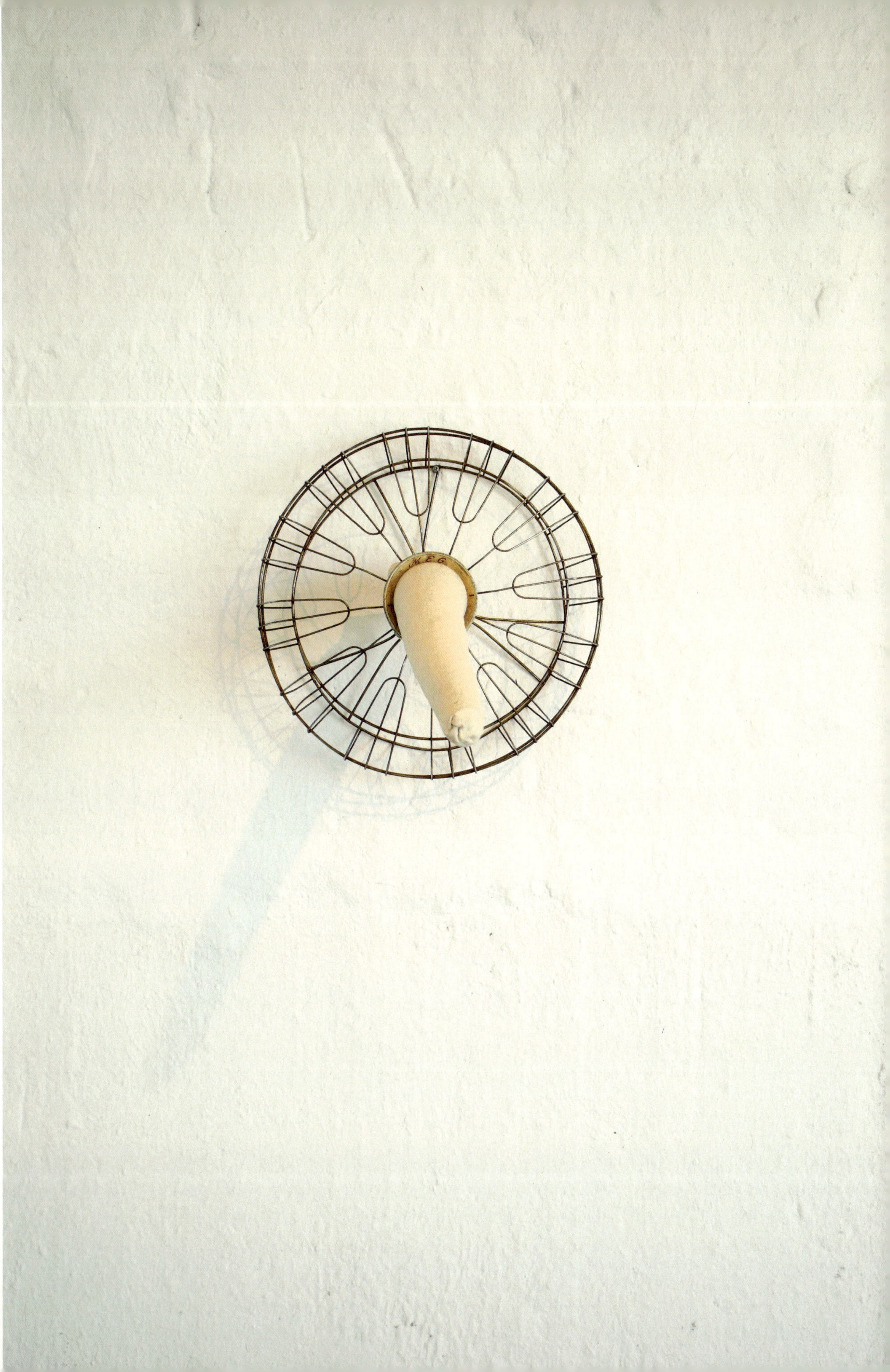

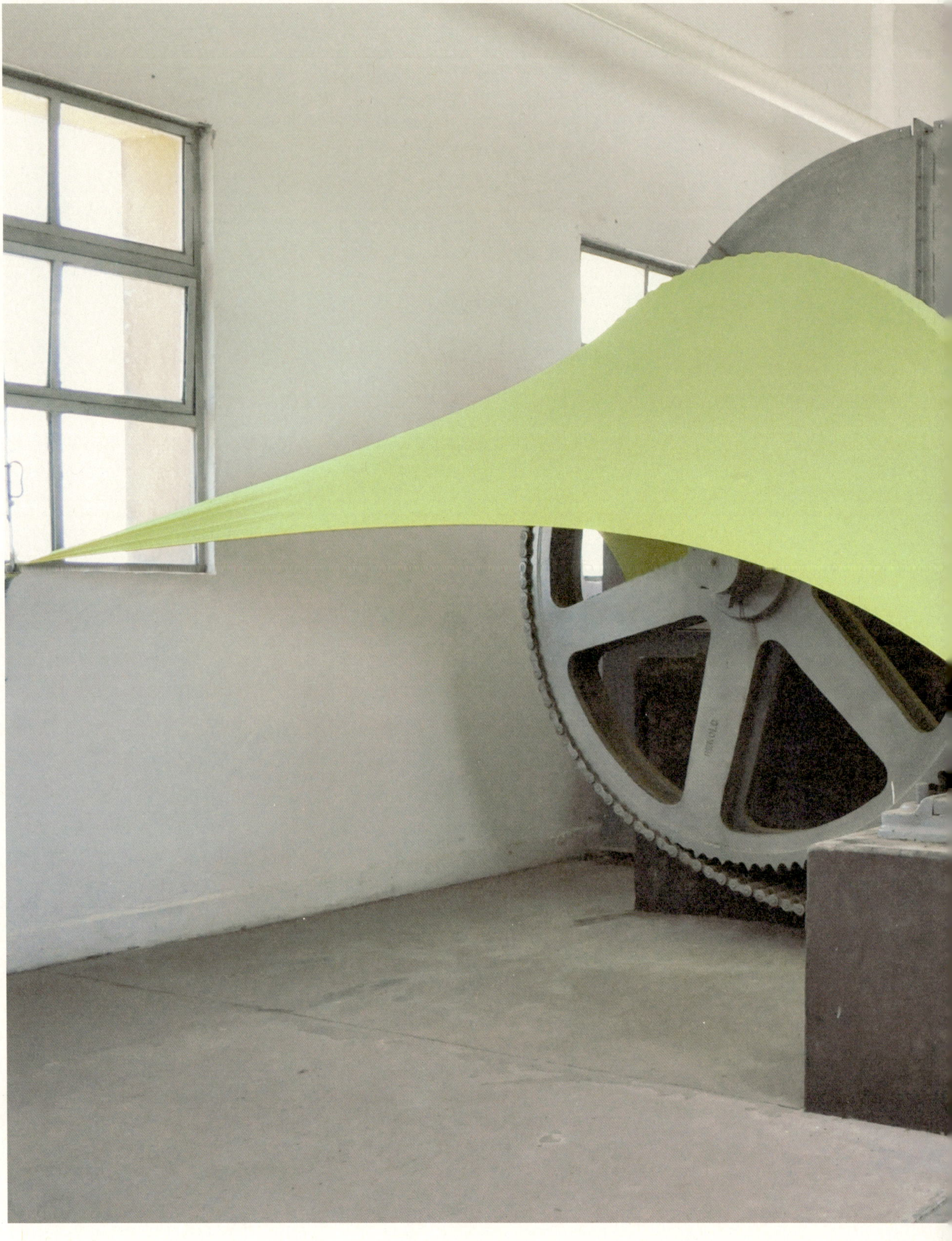

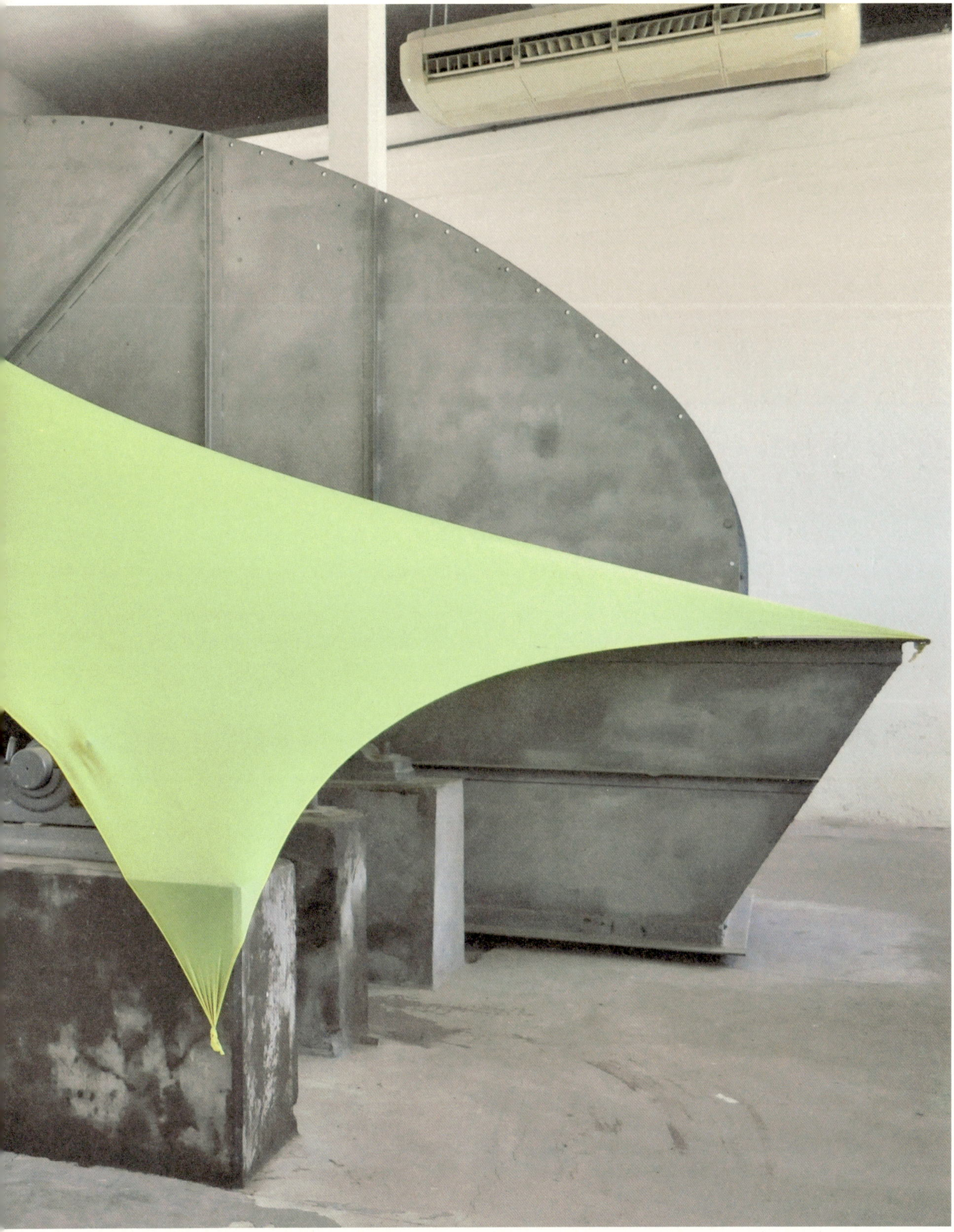

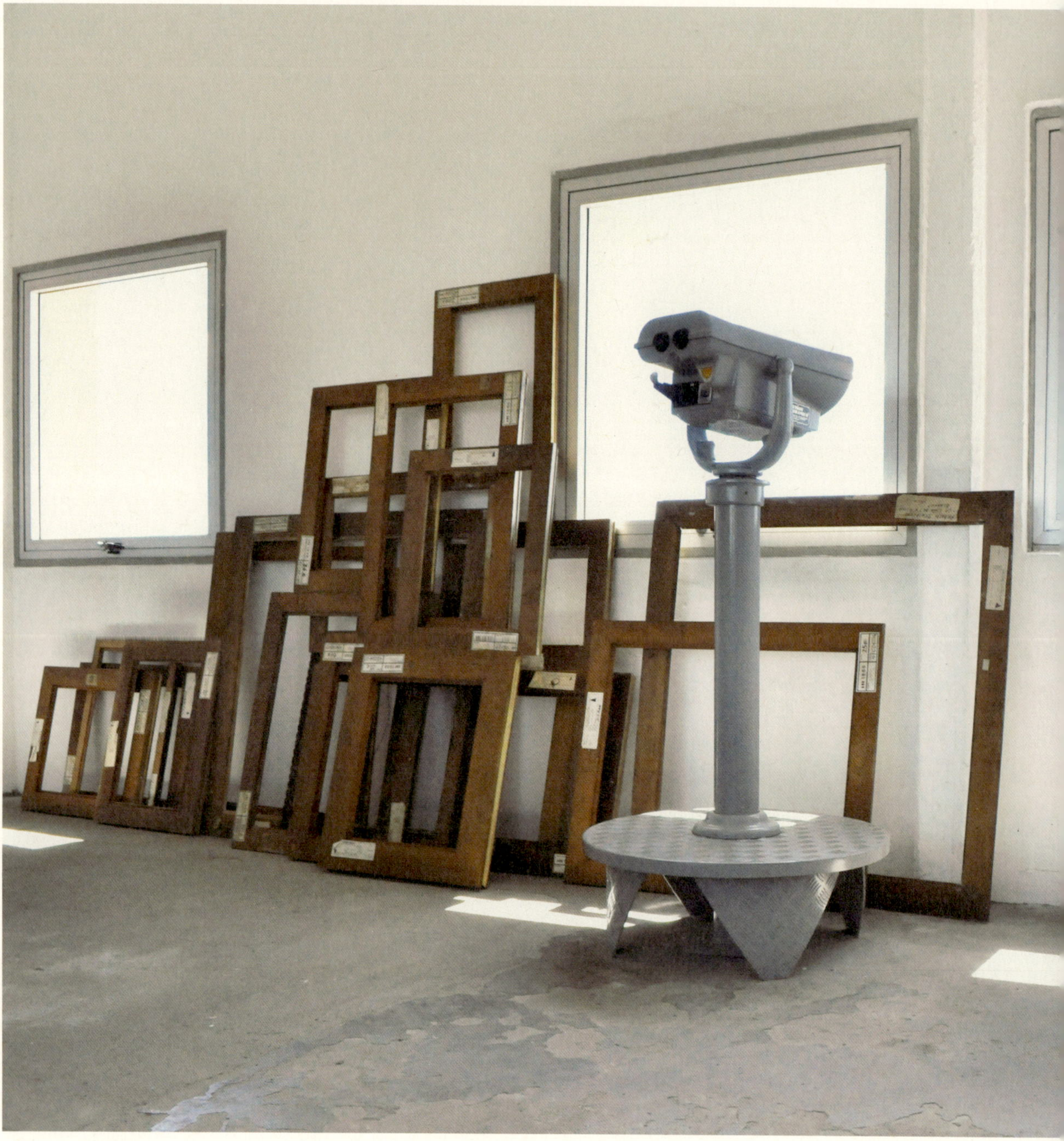

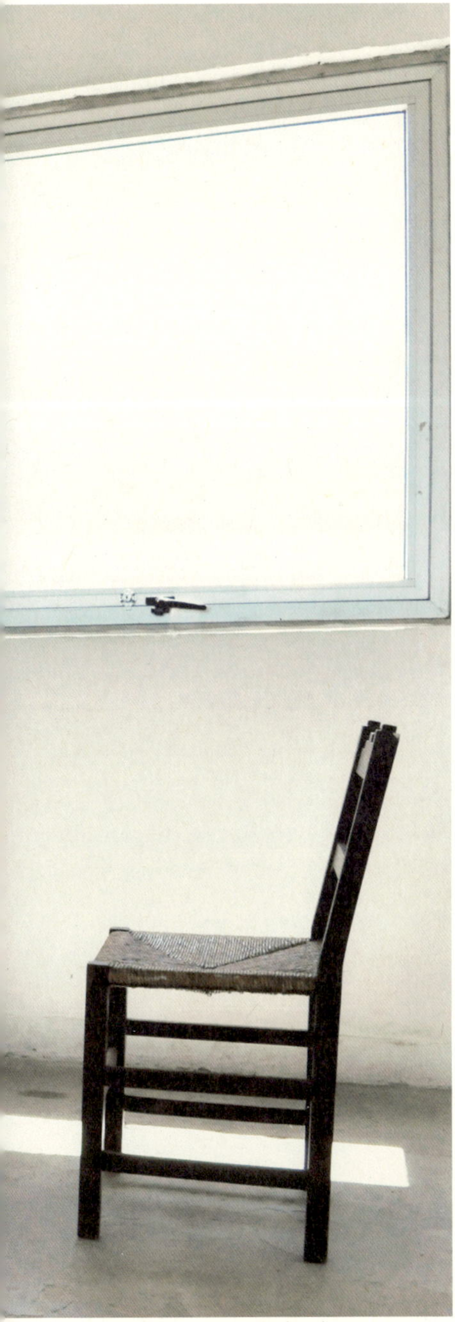

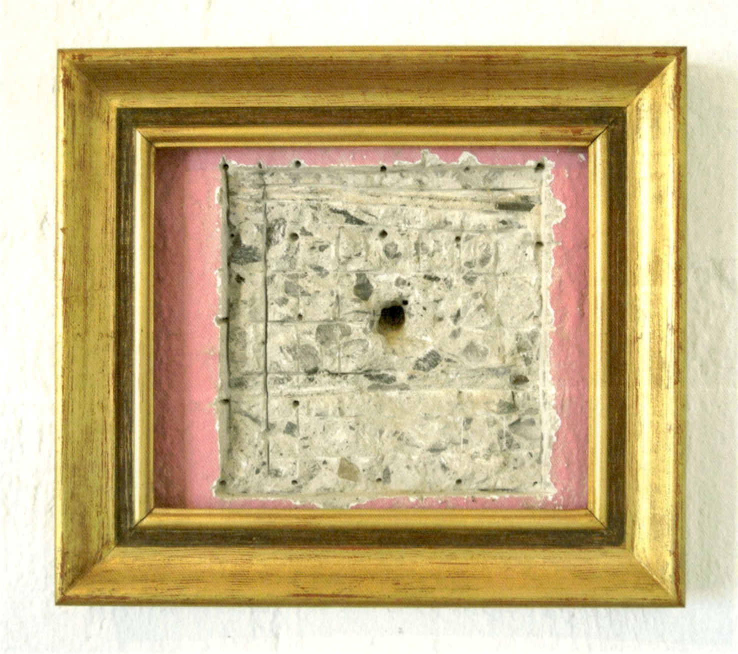

Ushuaia   Museo Marítimo

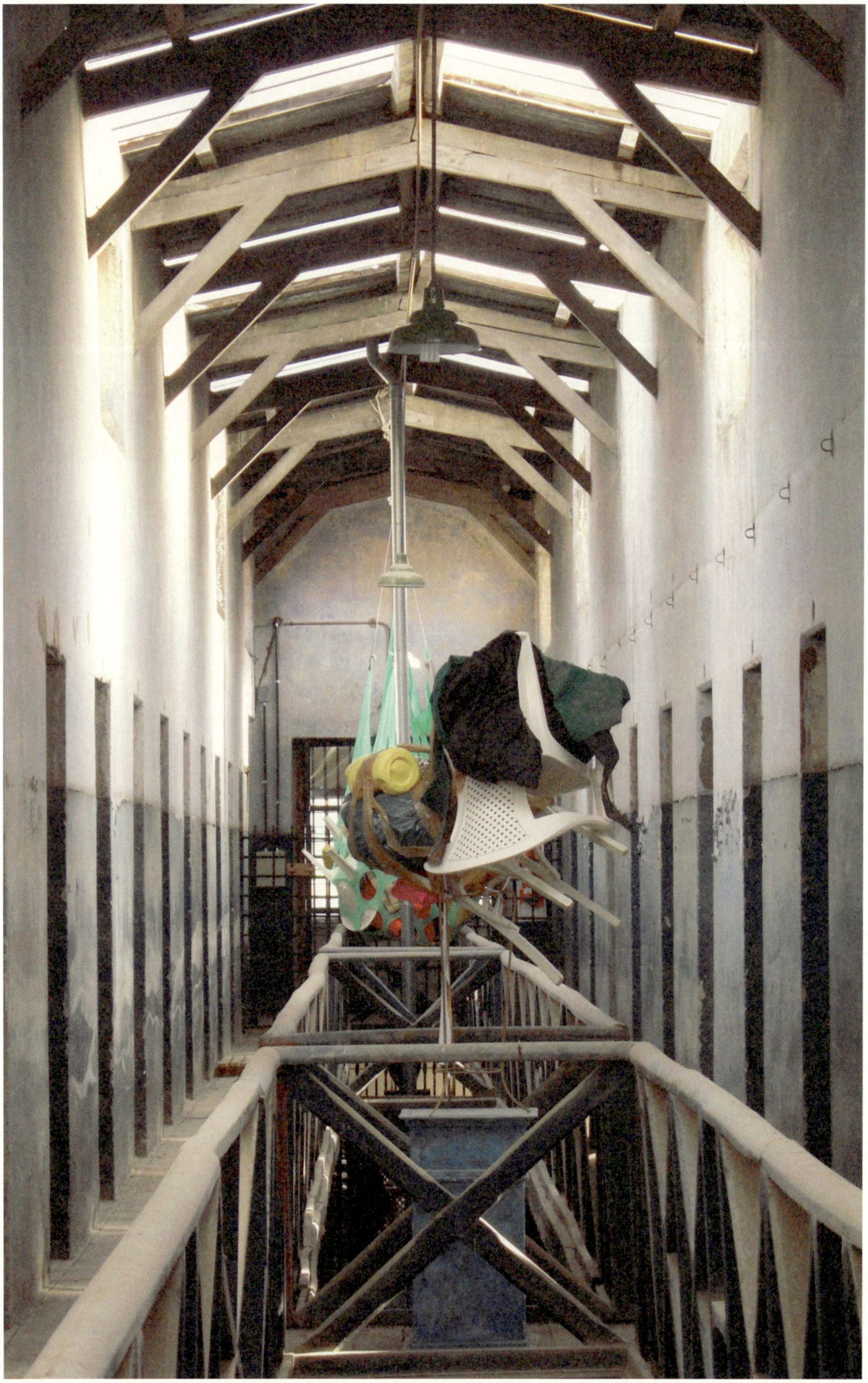

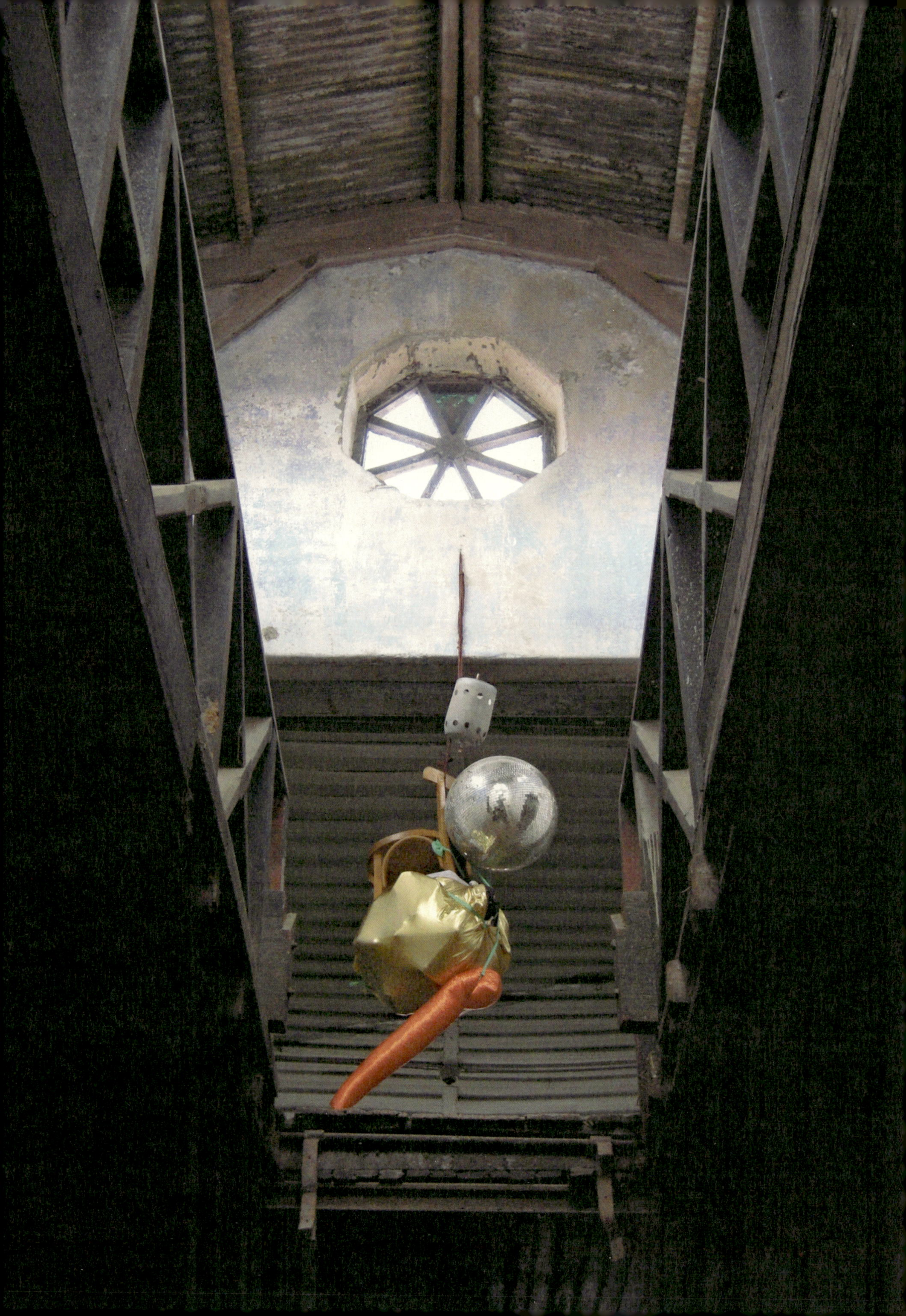

97　Ushuaia　Museo Marítimo

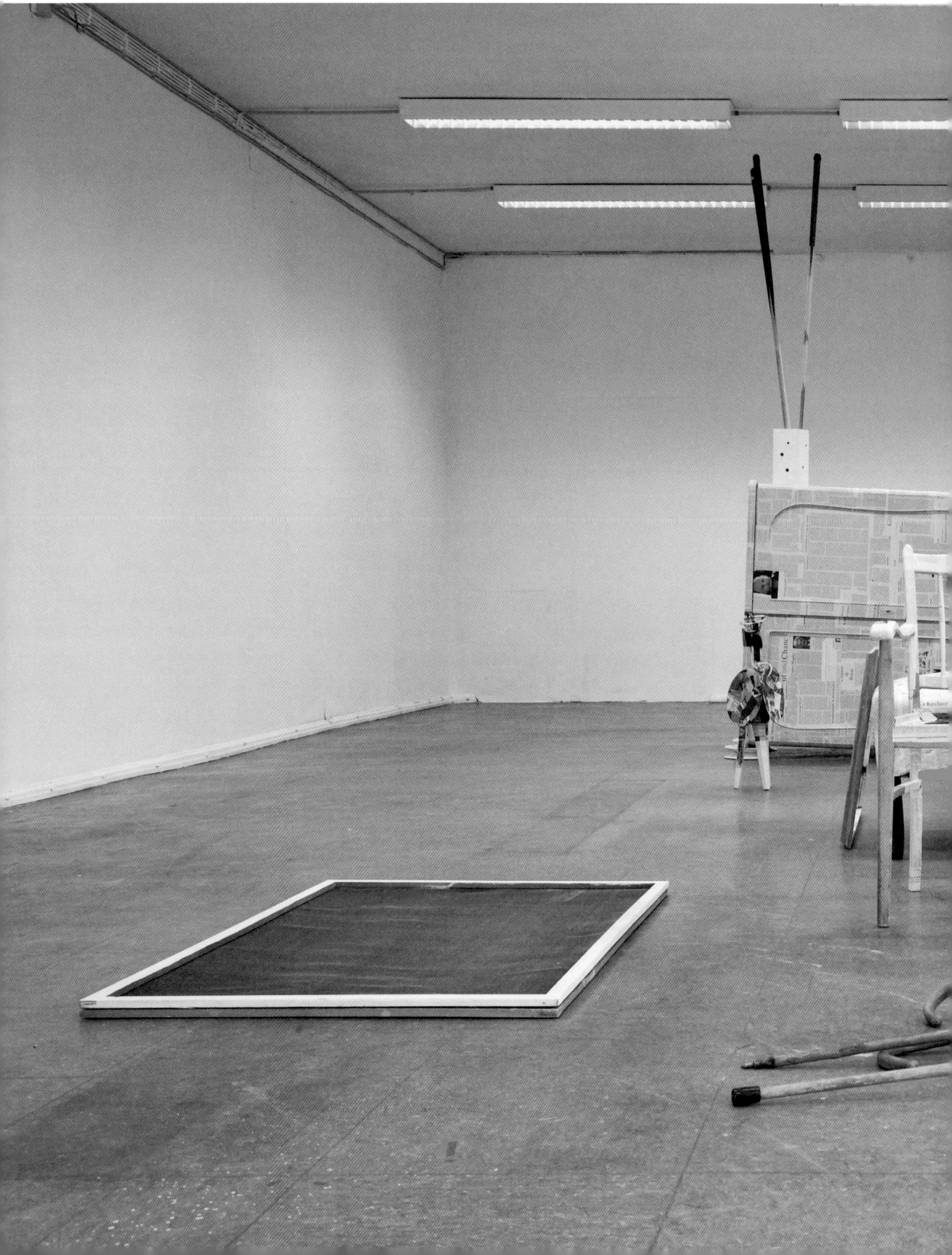

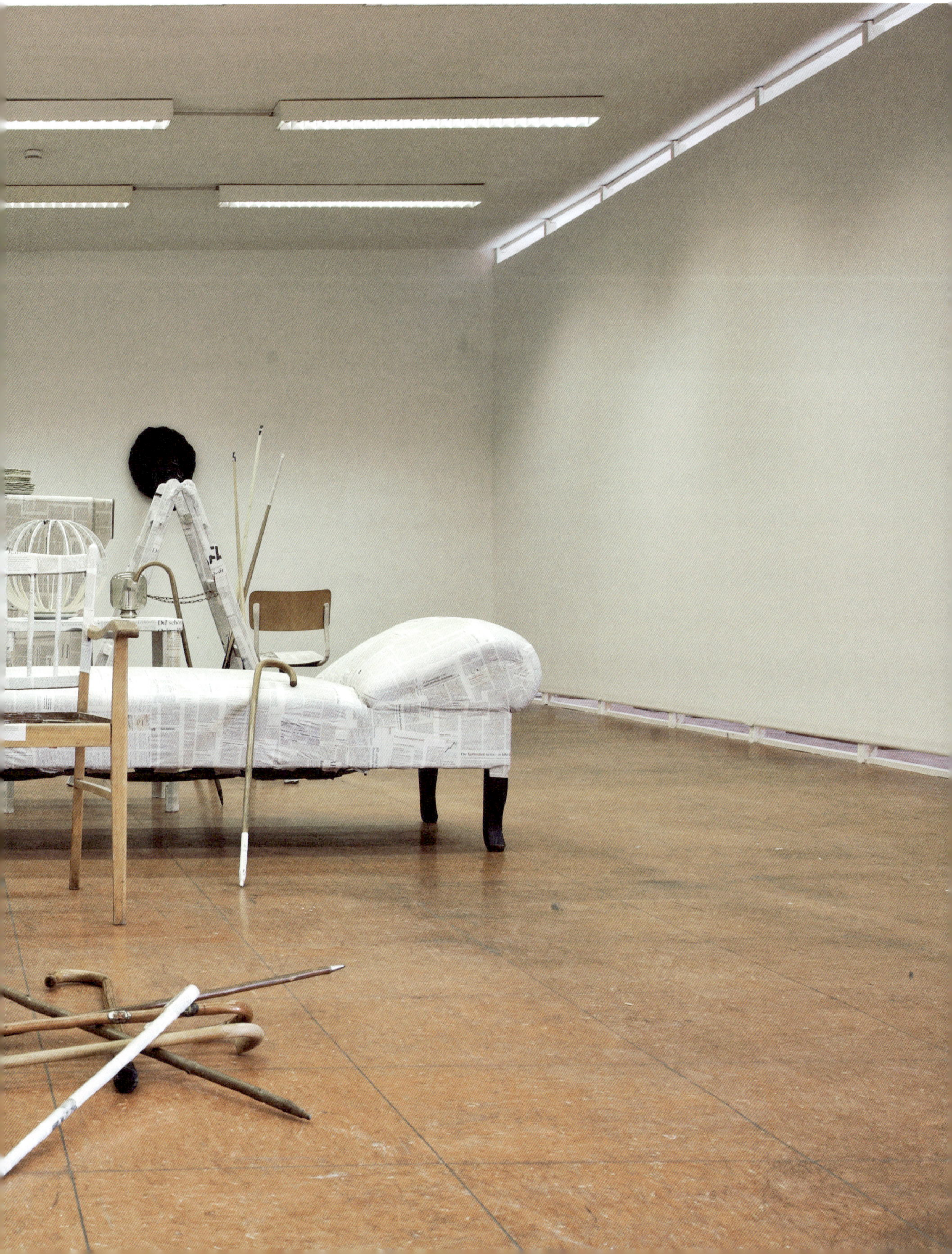

100 FRANKFURT ATELIERFRANKFURT

The Archive in the Worm

Andrés Duprat

The artist, who lives and works in Argentina and Germany, undertakes a creative journey across two continents, eight cities, and thousands of kilometers. The intention: a radical experience that utilizes objects from each place.

"Amid the pile of junk on the platform, Mele placed a slight folding chair that would serve as his sculpture's initial support. Using an arsenal of colored tapes, he began strapping items to the chair: first smaller stuffed plastic bags, then objects including old mops, buckets, furniture, fabrics, broken frames, boxes, and cans. Initially his actions were deliberate, and he paused occasionally to observe himself working on screen. As the shape began to grow, his movements became faster, frantic, and even violent. Mele picked up a chair and began to saw it. After struggling with it for a while, he smashed the chair on the ground and added the broken pieces to the work. At times running, he circled the sculpture with rounds of tape, kicking smaller objects out of the way. He finally dragged it off the platform, flipped it upside down onto a small wooden box, tightened and stabilized it with more objects and tape. The legs of the stool that were the work's initial foundation could now be seen jutting out of one side. After about 15 minutes of focused and physical work, the strange form became coherent. Mele gave it a final round of tape, jammed a walking stick into its soft center, and draped a stretcher bar over the top like a frame. He briefly considered the finished work, gathered his suit coat, and joined the public."

[Fragment of a text by Emi Winter and Steffen Böddeker written on the occasion of Martín Mele´s performance in 2007 at the Museo de Arte Contemporáneo, Oaxaca, Mexico]

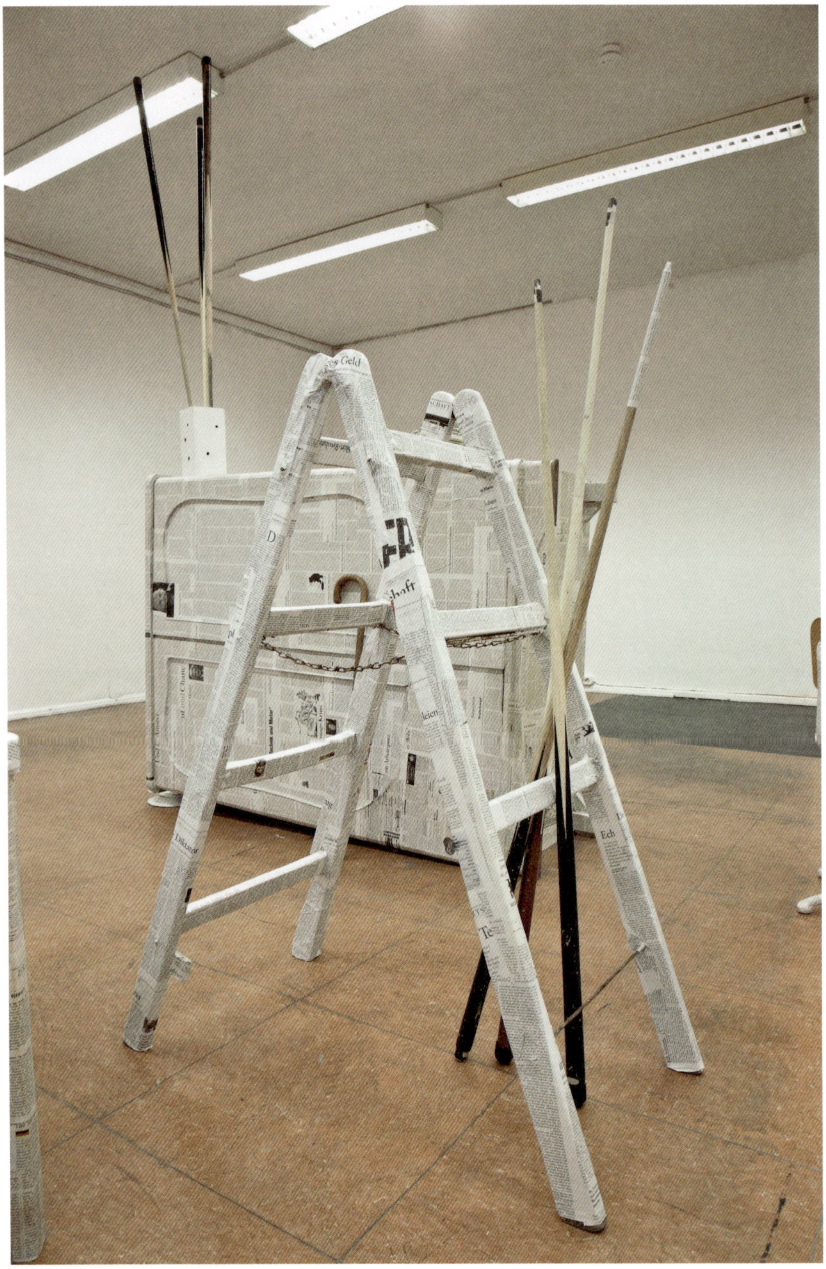

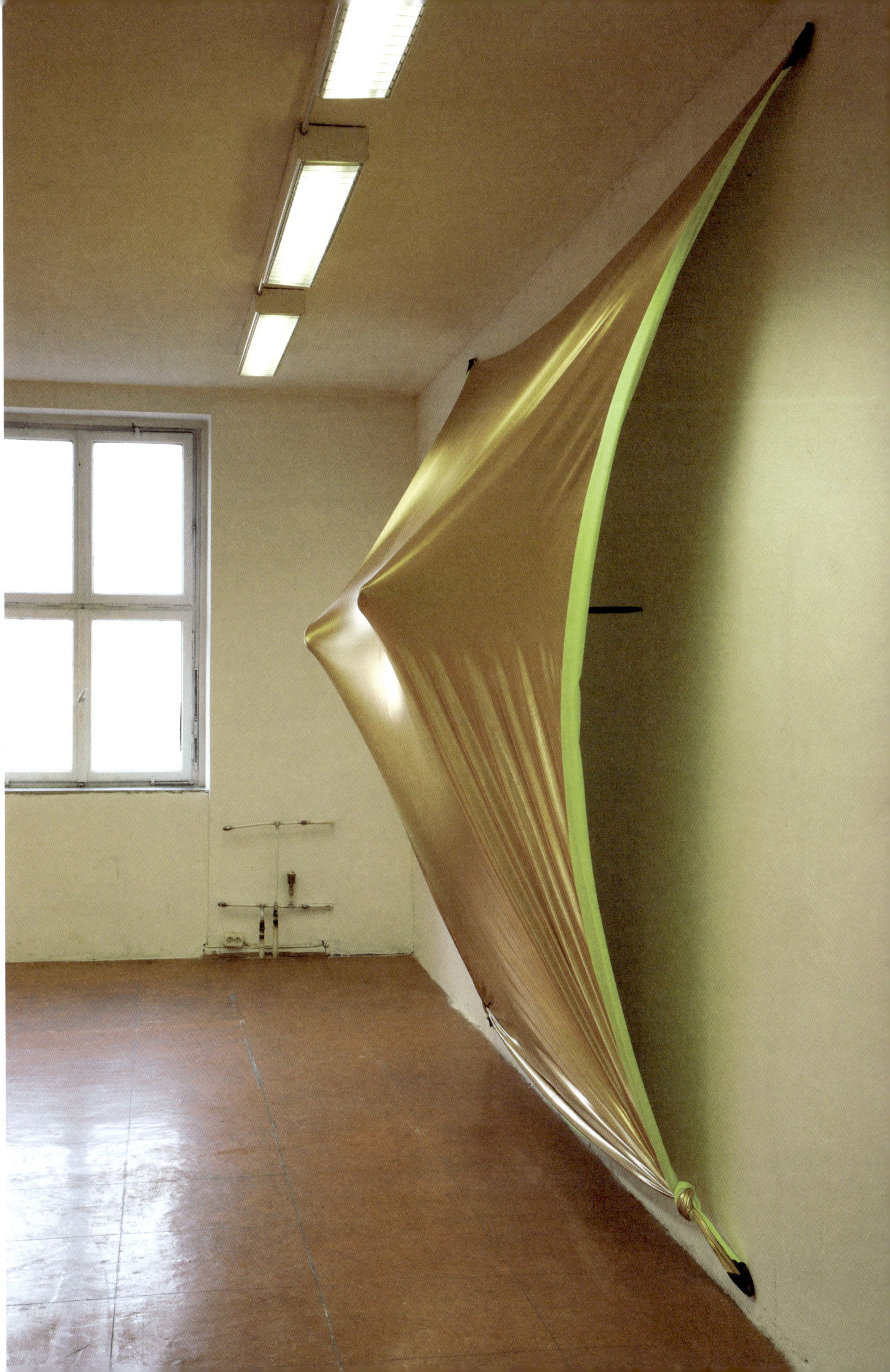

The intention behind this project by Argentinean artist Martín Mele (born in Buenos Aires, 1960) is based on a central concept: travel as an experience. The project exceeds the format of the exhibition or performance, and even goes beyond what we would usually call a travelling show. At issue is a radical experience, not without risk, capable of exerting an influence in a determinant form during the genesis of the work, an action that operates directly within the work of art's system of creation and production.

With *The Archive in the Worm*, Mele embarks on a journey – both in a physical and spiritual sense – involving two continents, eight cities, and an itinerary of thousands of kilometers. In this way, the works transform into actions, influenced by this continuous movement. And art is generated at the intersections among experience, the dialog with each realm of his adventures and the quality of the objects.

Conceived in two stages, this project, which has the support of Argentina's Secretaría de Cultura de la Nación and the Kulturstiftung NRW, in Germany, proposes a method of working that is defined by way of two determinant decisions: a point of departure and an established geographical itinerary. In the first stage, Mele undertakes a veritable *tour de force* a month in duration, traveling, collecting, creating and presenting his works in four cities in Argentina: Salta, Rosario, Neuquén and Ushuaia. He plans this exercise like a field of aesthetic experimentation where empiricism is the method, and consequently the result is unpredictable.

      The artist gathers, assembles, places, corrects, breaks, dismantles: his instruments are thus his gaze, his reflections, his skills, his instinct, his convictions, his trials, and of course, his errors, his blunder, doubts, and coincidences. Everything is visible, all is shown, the intention is to evoke experience in the objects. And, once expressed the work, a certain loss of what has been experienced becomes evident which remains as a vestige, like mute testimony.

      In this way Mele exposes the genesis of his ideas, his discoveries and his wanderings to public view. He transforms the exhibition hall into an open workshop, in this way undermining established social practices, such as the idea of exhibiting a finished work, the official opening, the roles of the audience and the creators, the concepts of the spectator and the spectacle, the meaningfulness of the artist working alone. He makes surprising connections, in so doing conferring to his work an unusual social dimension. His objects come alive because they create links: they highlight social and material links on the stage of life. They are the condensed experience of social and material facts.

By expanding his action in the encounter of the exhibition space with this artistic experience and his perceptions and personal imagination, the work is generated in and through this unique and particular contact. Within the course of a single month, February 2010, Mele developed and presented his works at the Museo de Bellas Artes de Salta, the Museo de Arte Contemporáneo in Rosario, and the Museo Nacional de Bellas Artes in Neuquén and in March 2010 he showed them at the Museo Marítimo de Ushuaia. Once the artist's action was concluded at each museum, the four shows remained open to the audience simultaneously, and could be visited during April.

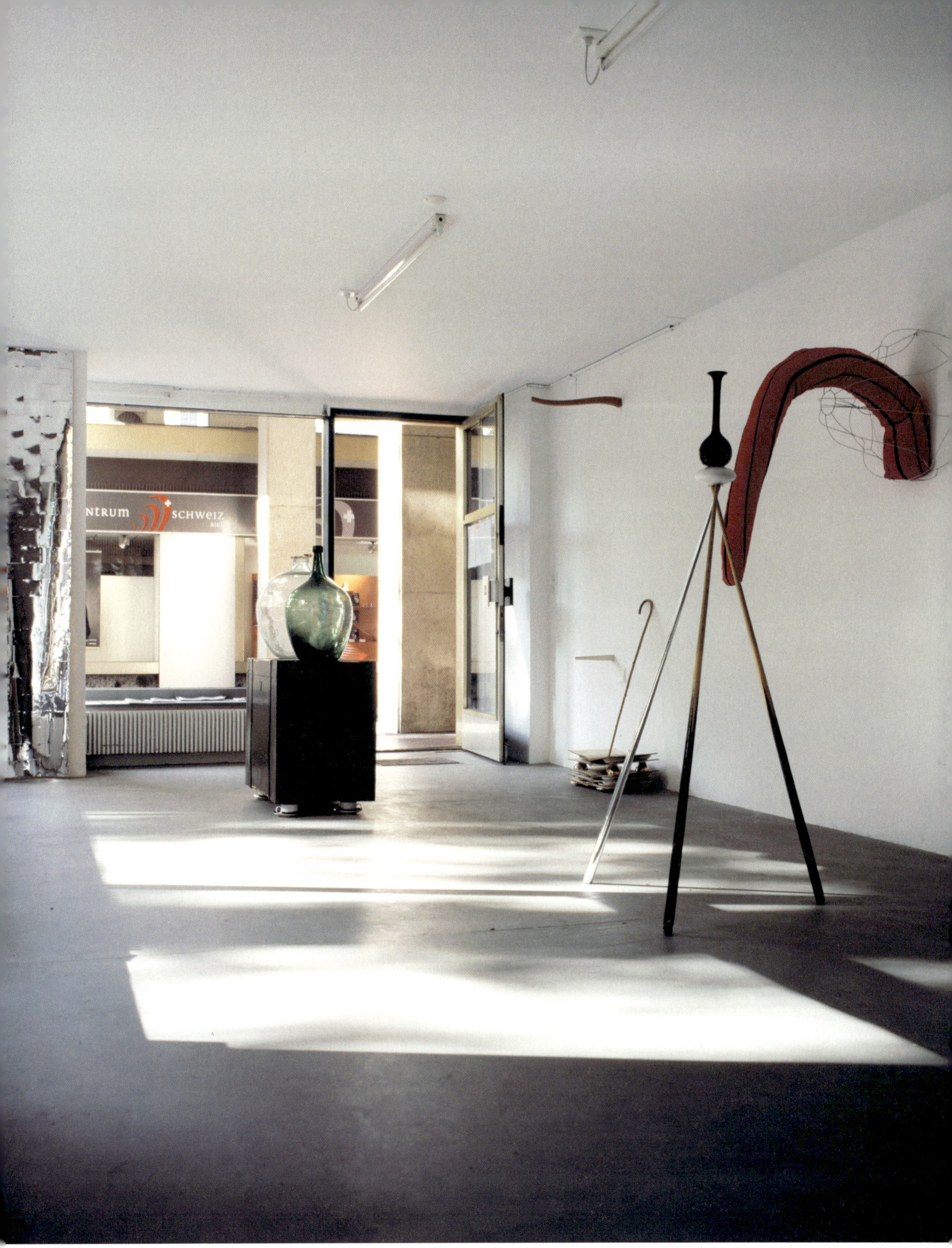
SCHWEIZ

The second stage, similar in its characteristics, winded up in Europe during the second half of 2010, involving institutions in Frankfurt, Biel, Berlin, and Neuss. The cycle is ended with the publishing of this book, bringing together and documenting the entire project.

Martin Mele's adventures between the two continents will offer different possibilities and generate diverse results that should then be seen in a specific relation to the city, the context, the characteristics of the exhibition space, and the circumstances that the artist confronted in each moment of his peregrinations. An inveterate traveler, an Argentinean raised in the Netherlands, and in the last 20 years residing alternately in Germany and Argentina, Mele embodies a perspective characterized by multiple journeys back and forth between Europe and America, a theme in Argentinean culture. It is his, however, a peculiar kind of travel with a restorative element, tinged with a personal dimension that inverts or at least questions the Borgian dictum, "We Argentineans are Europeans in exile".

The journey becomes pivotal to the exhibition: both for the artist and his numerous changes of location and for the objects that he collects, selects, moves, decontextualizes, manipulates, and distorts to create his works, constantly modifying in some way his origin, his path and his goal. The materials of Mele's works are the found objects lying by the wayside. And *The Archive in the Worm* attests to what remains when time has eroded the mountain of experience: the worm has devoured the archive. Mele proposes that we take a good look at the result. The archive is his personal memory.

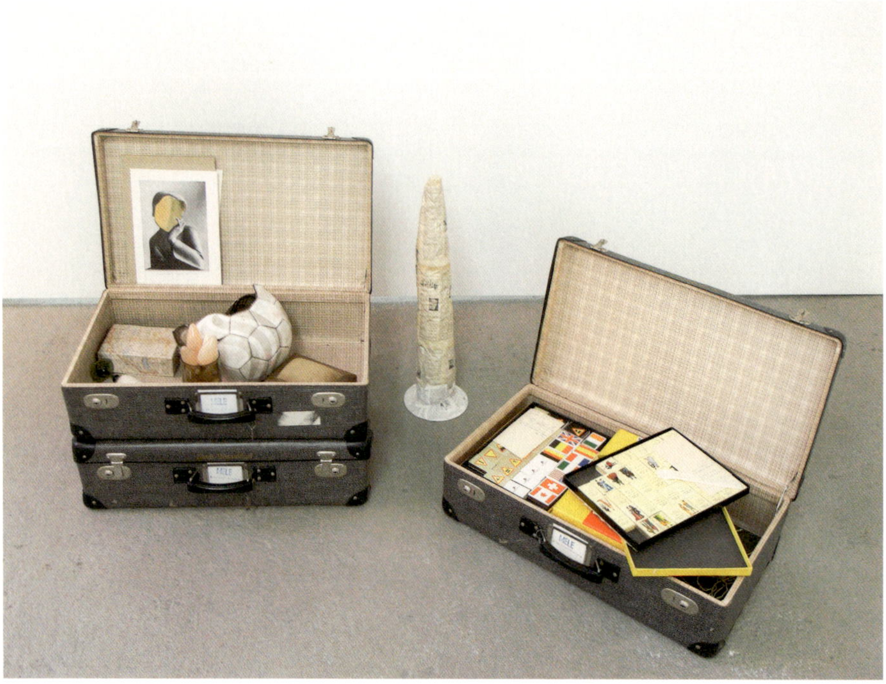

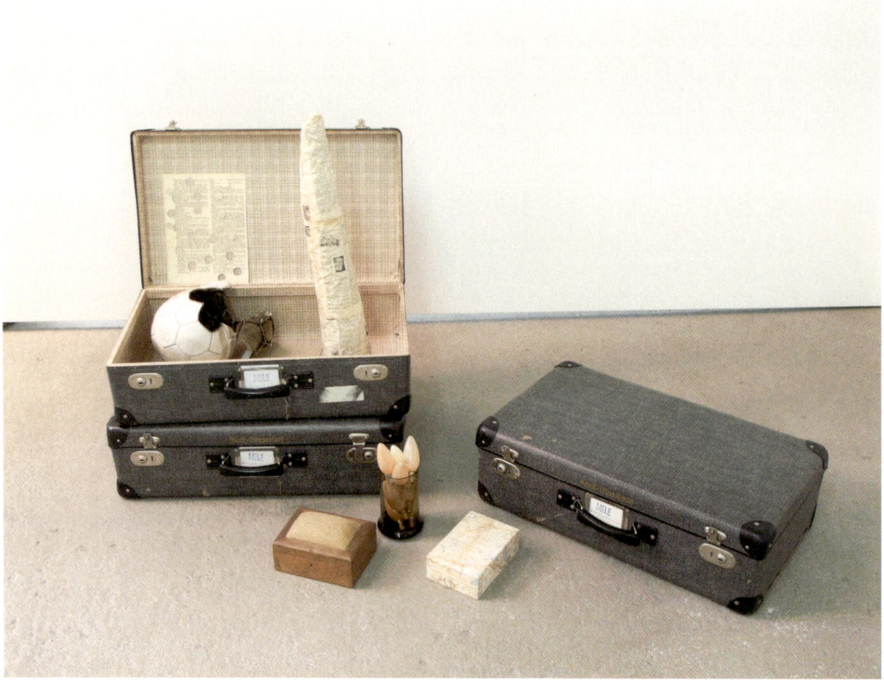

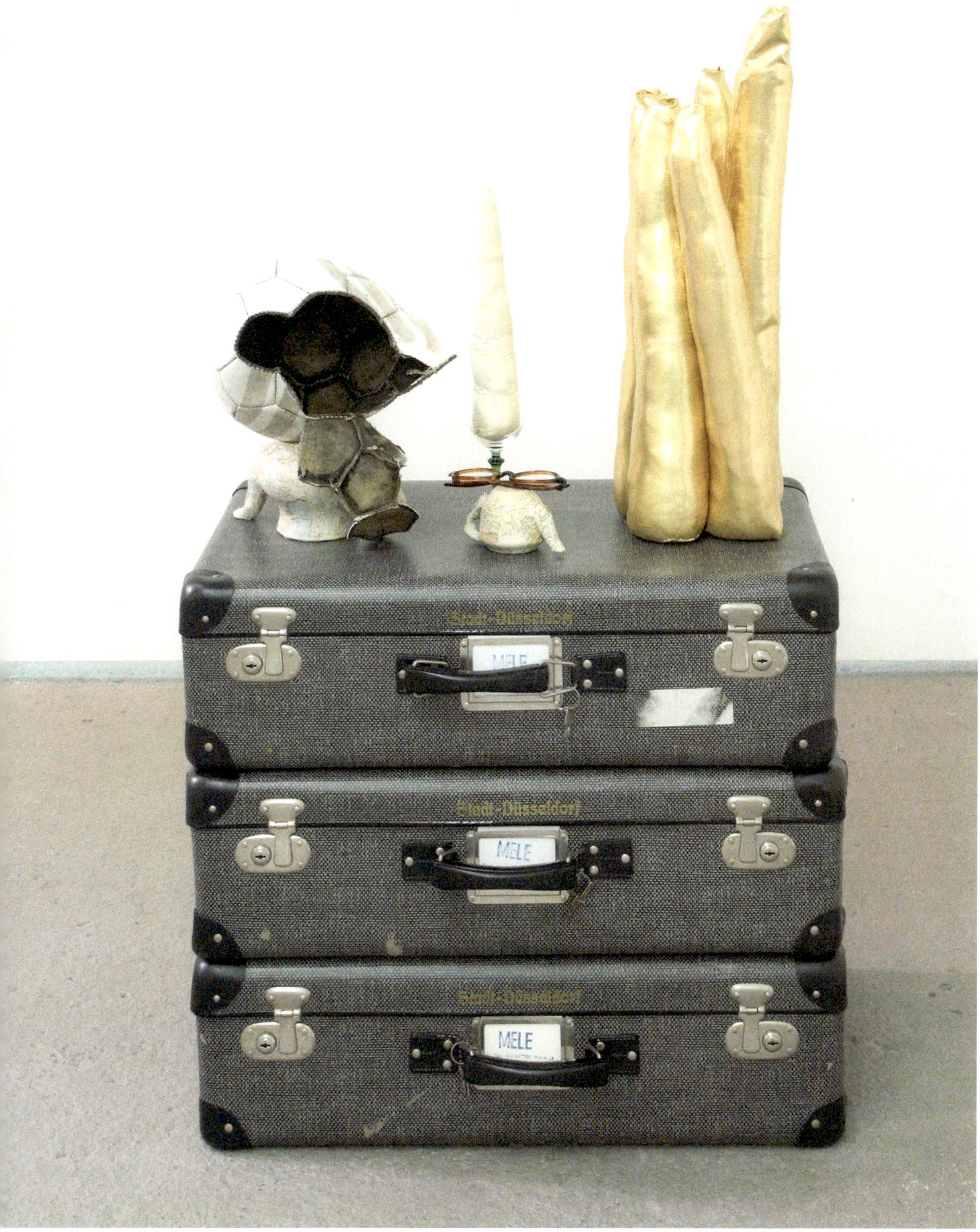
MELE
MELE
MELE

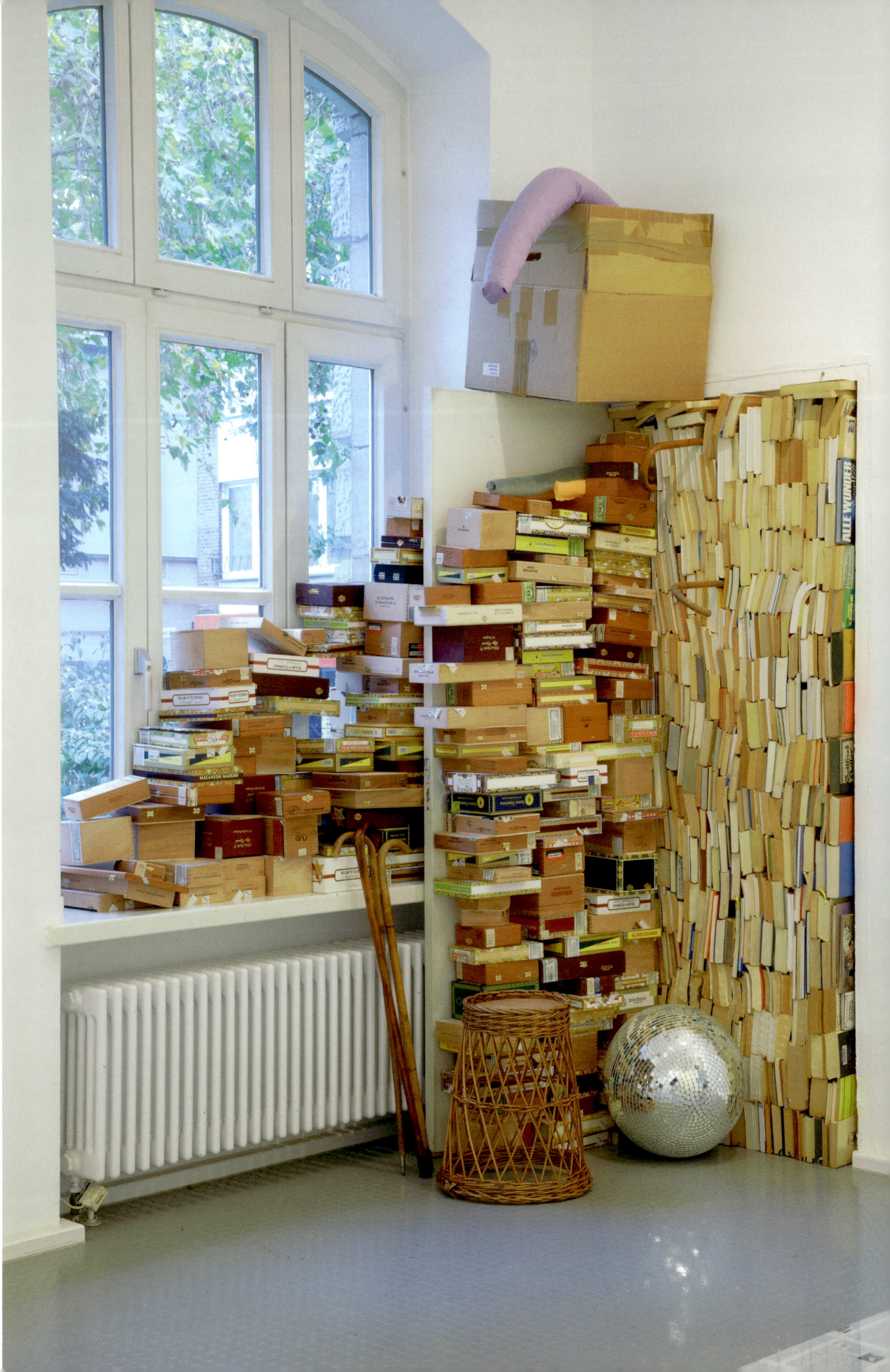
ALLE WUNDER

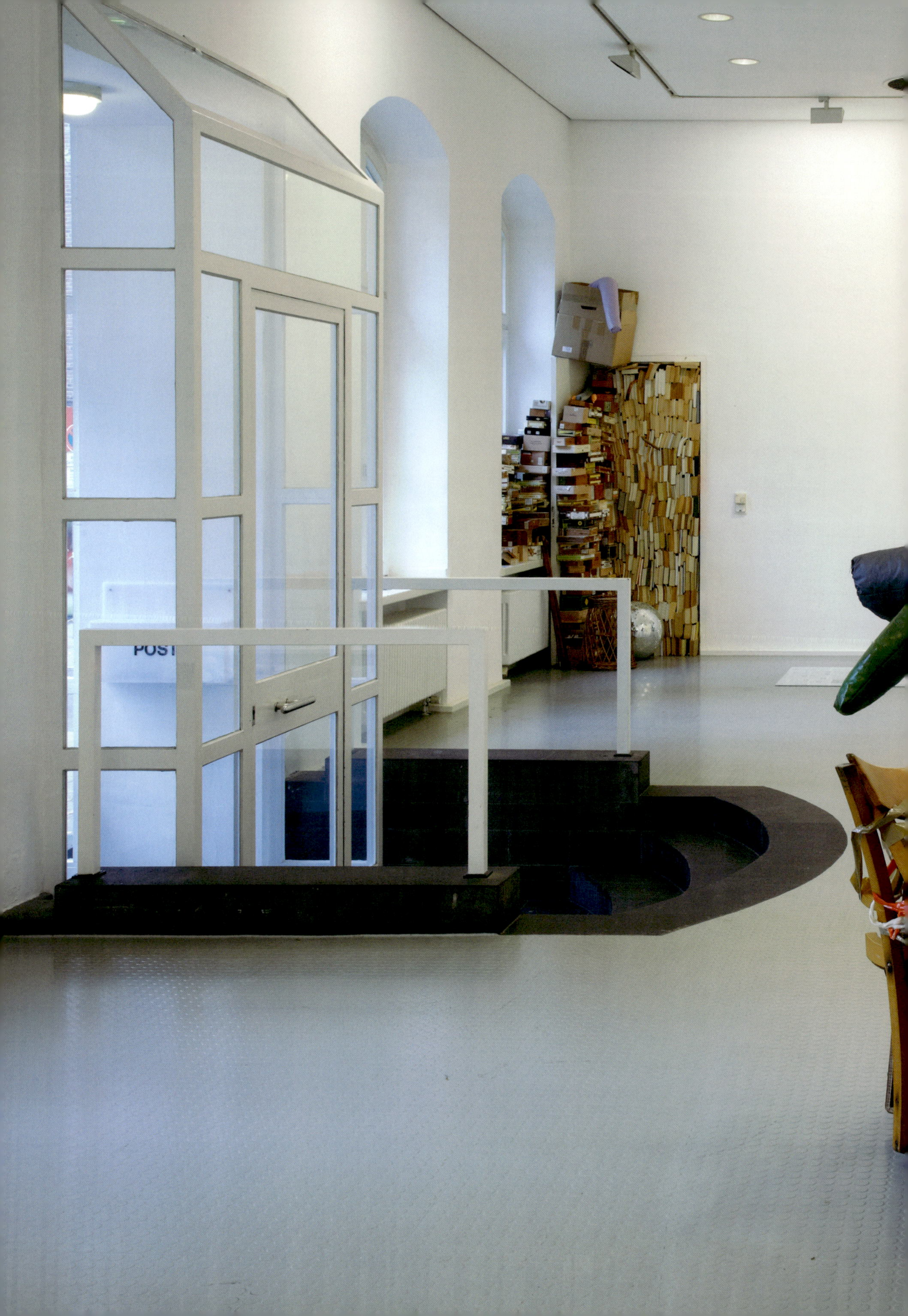
POST

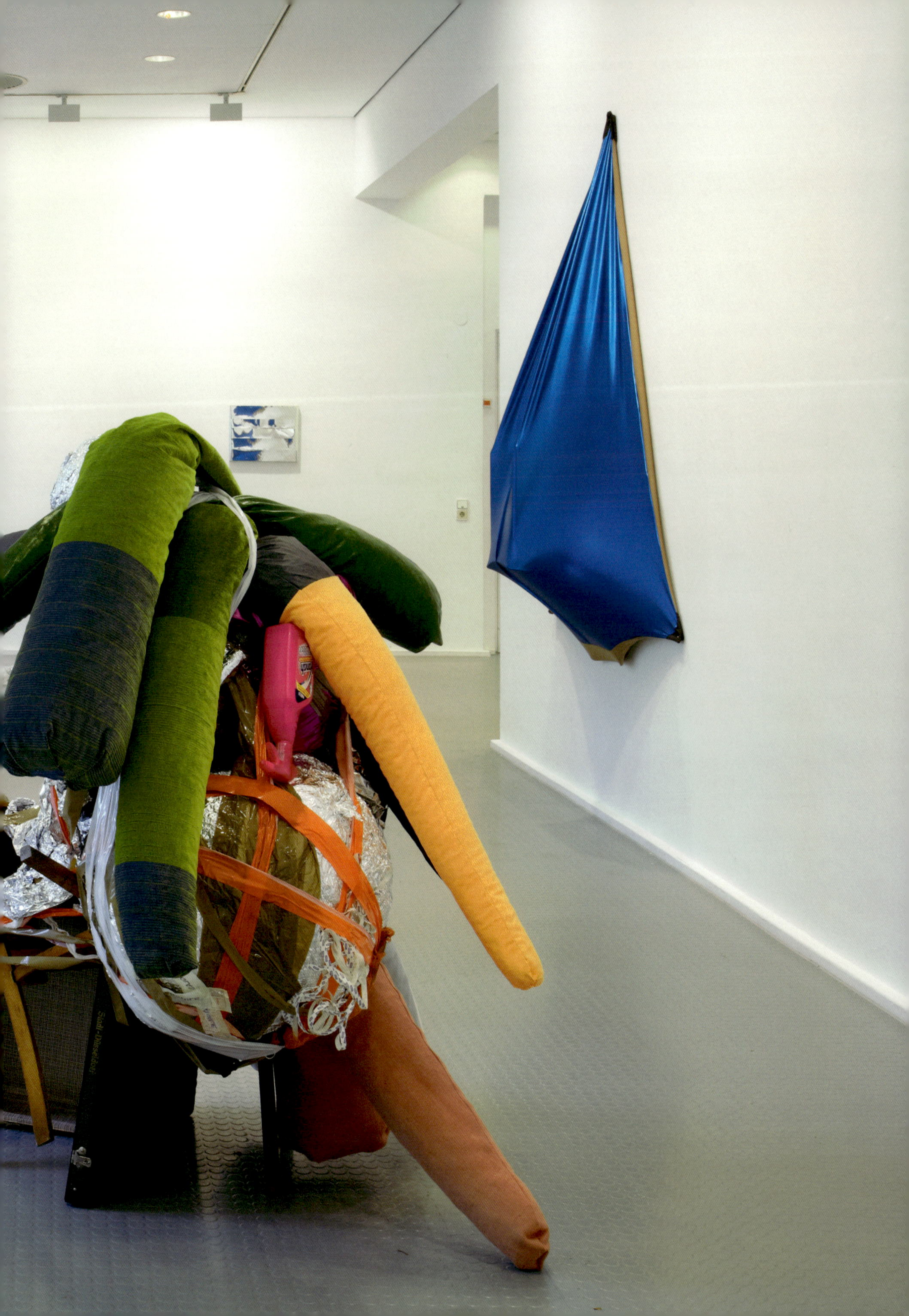

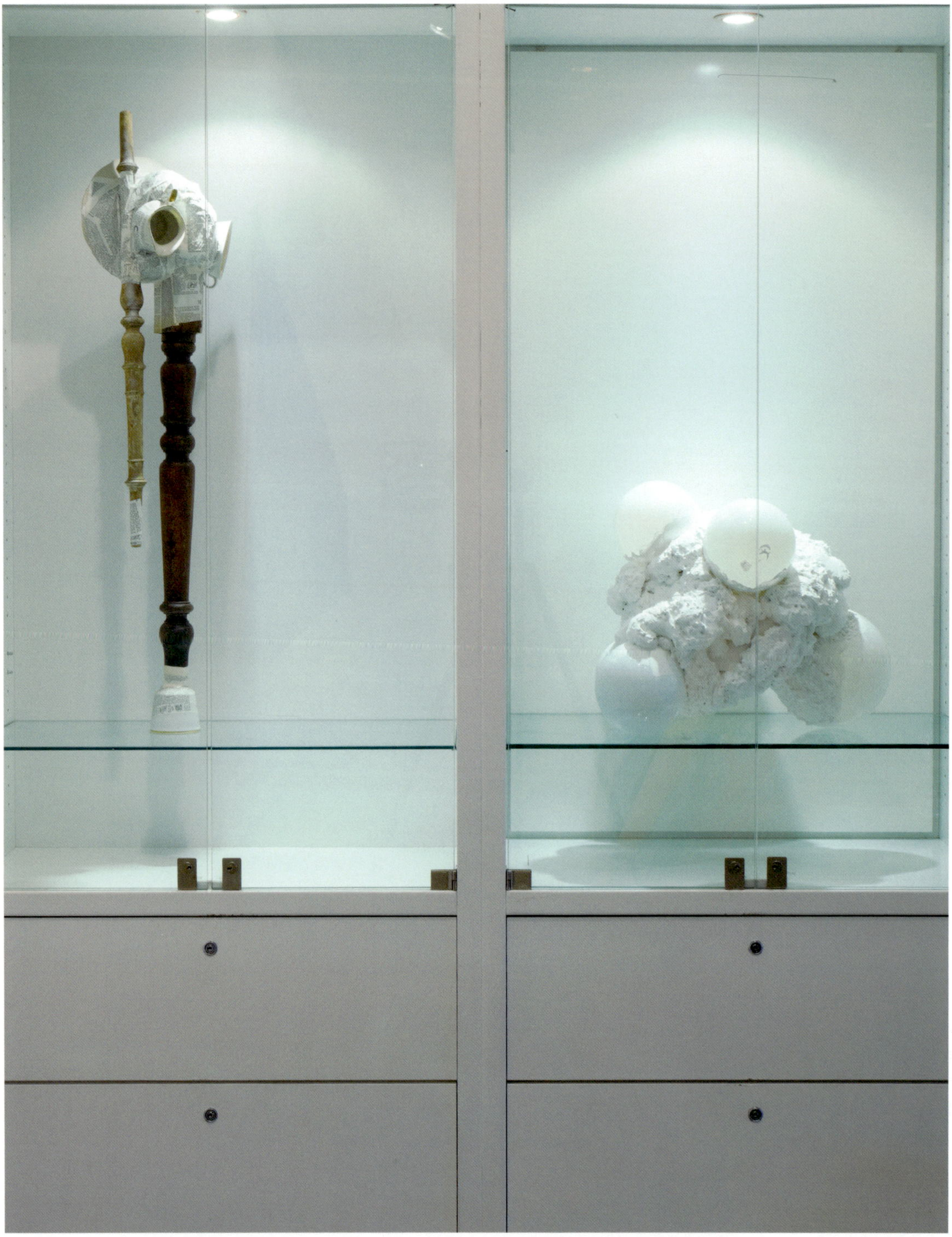

117

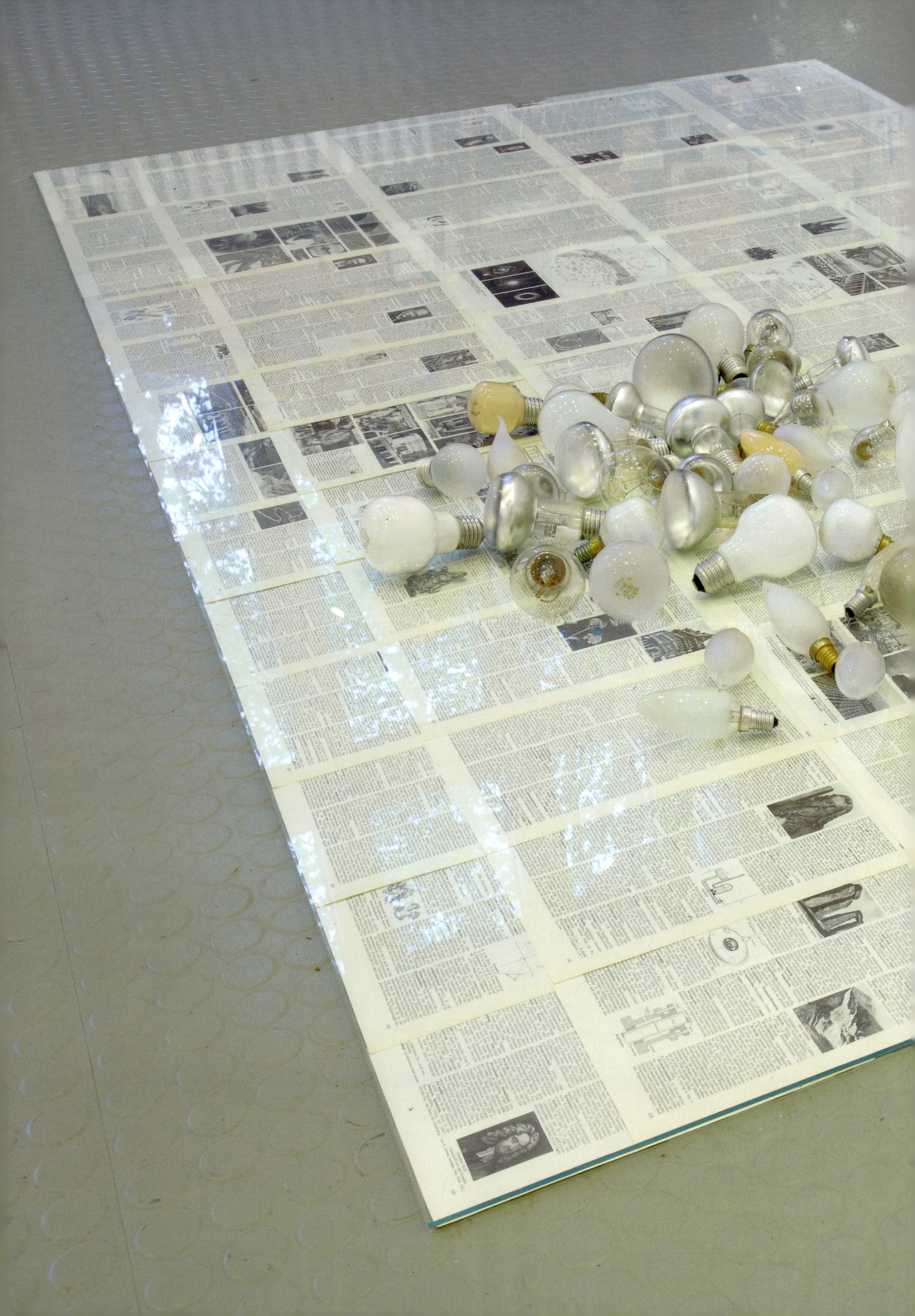

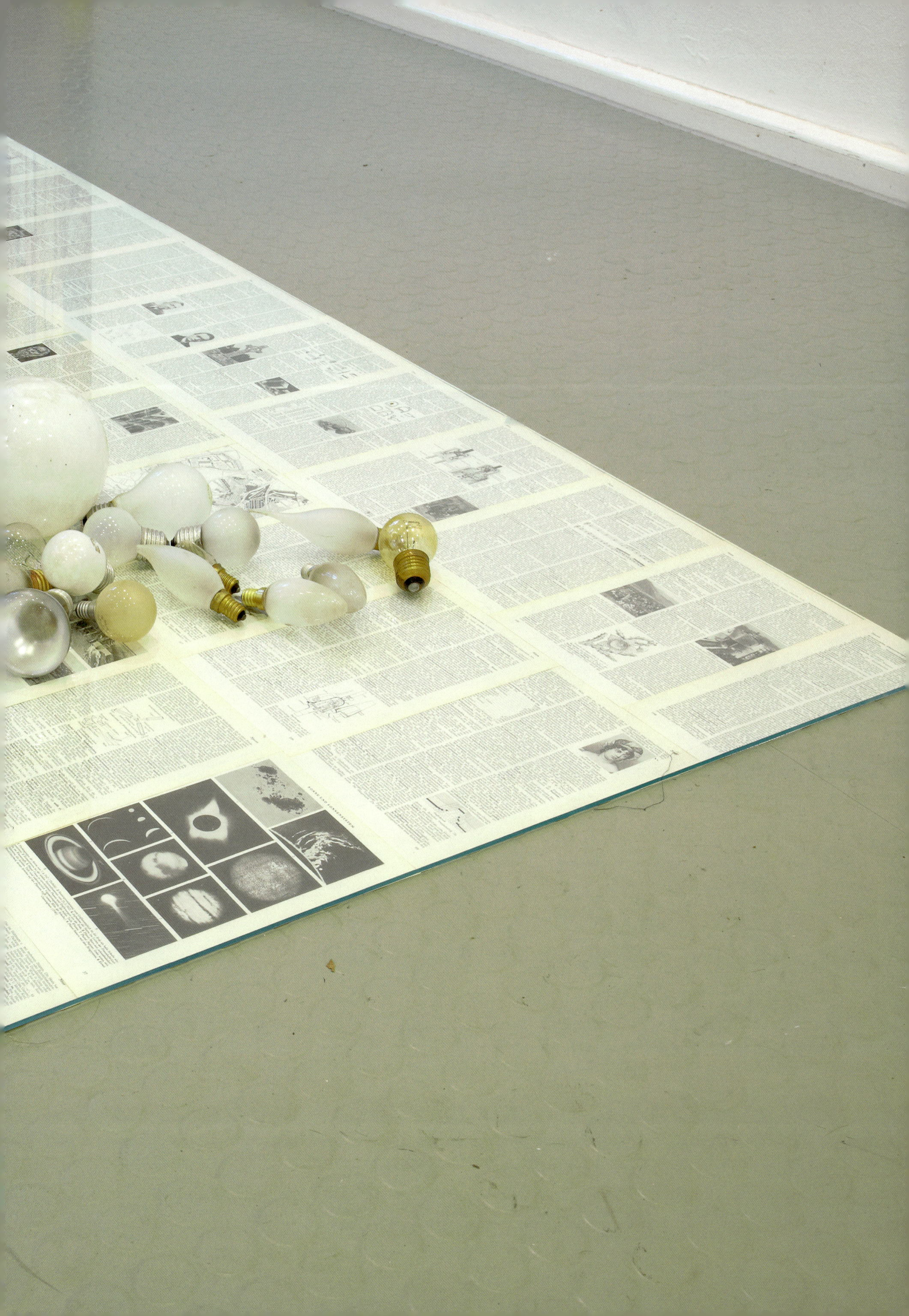

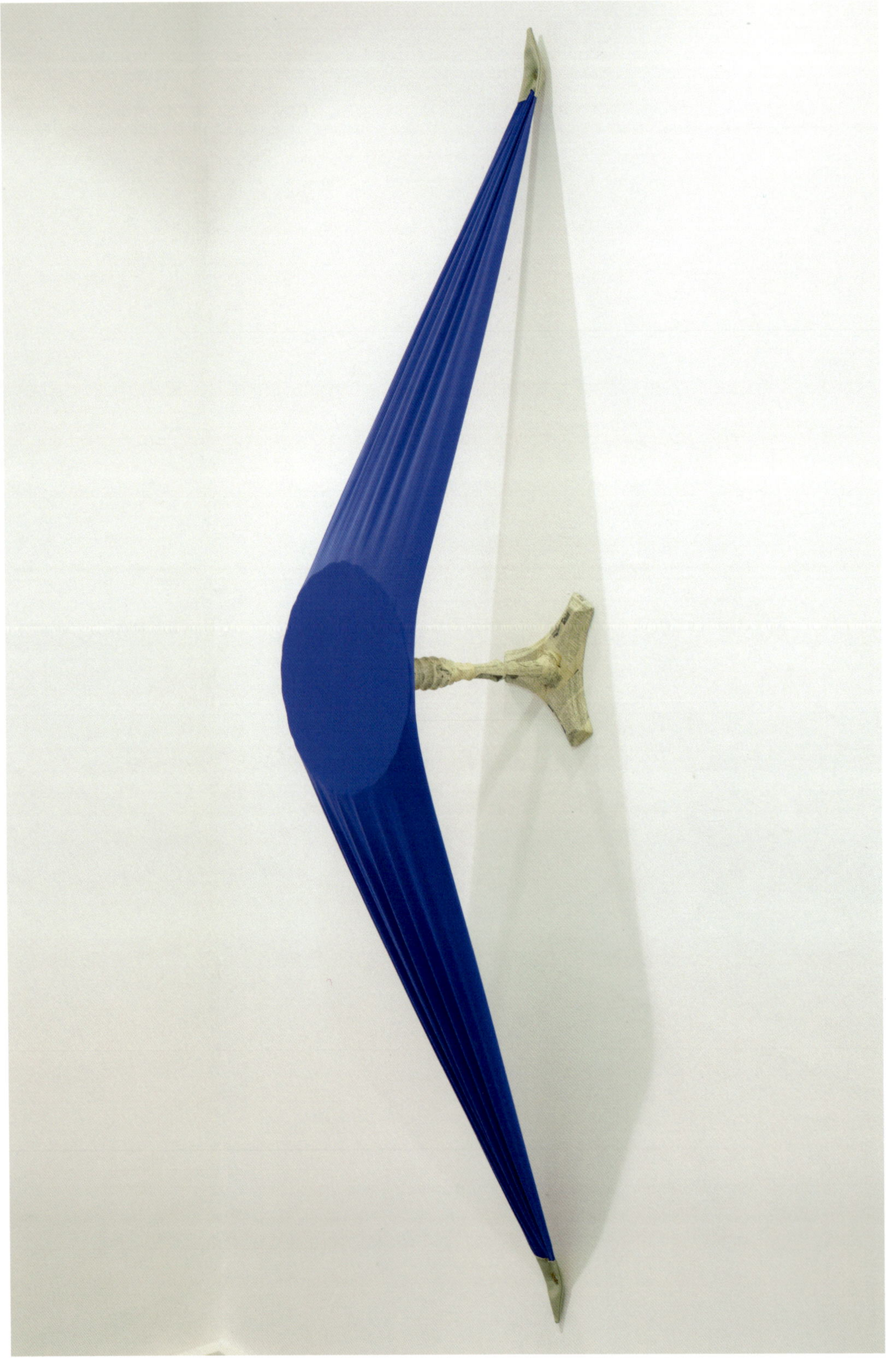

121

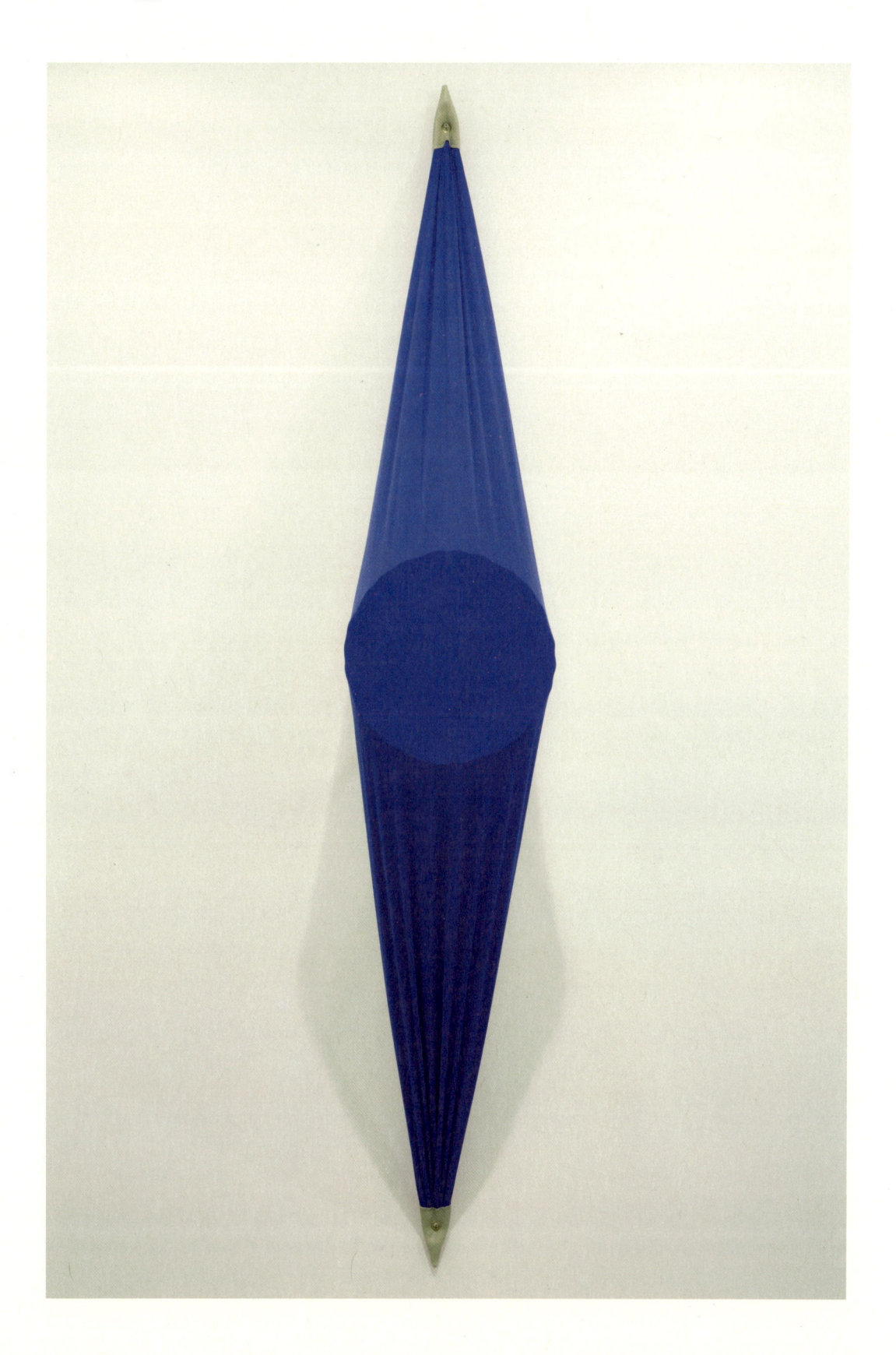

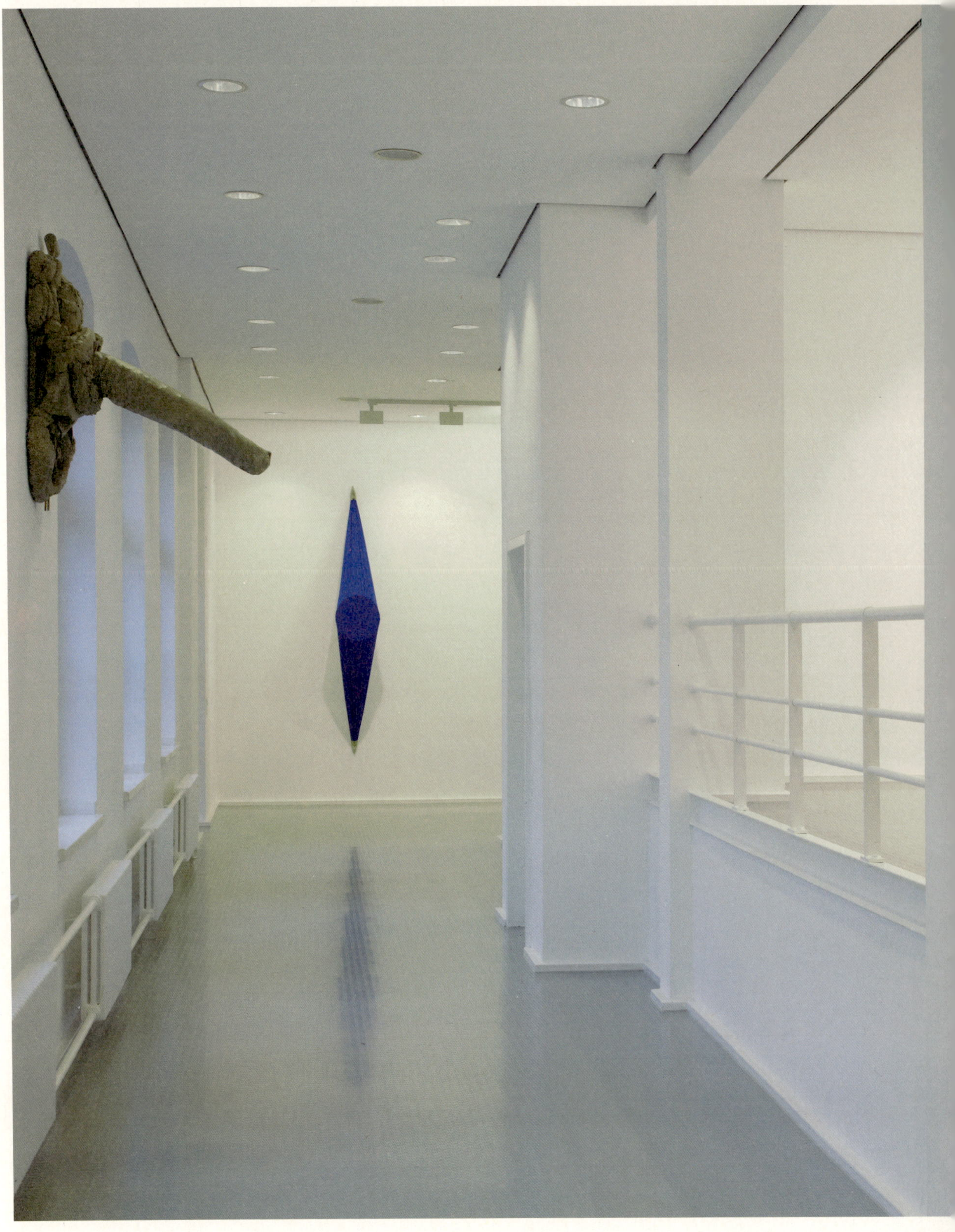

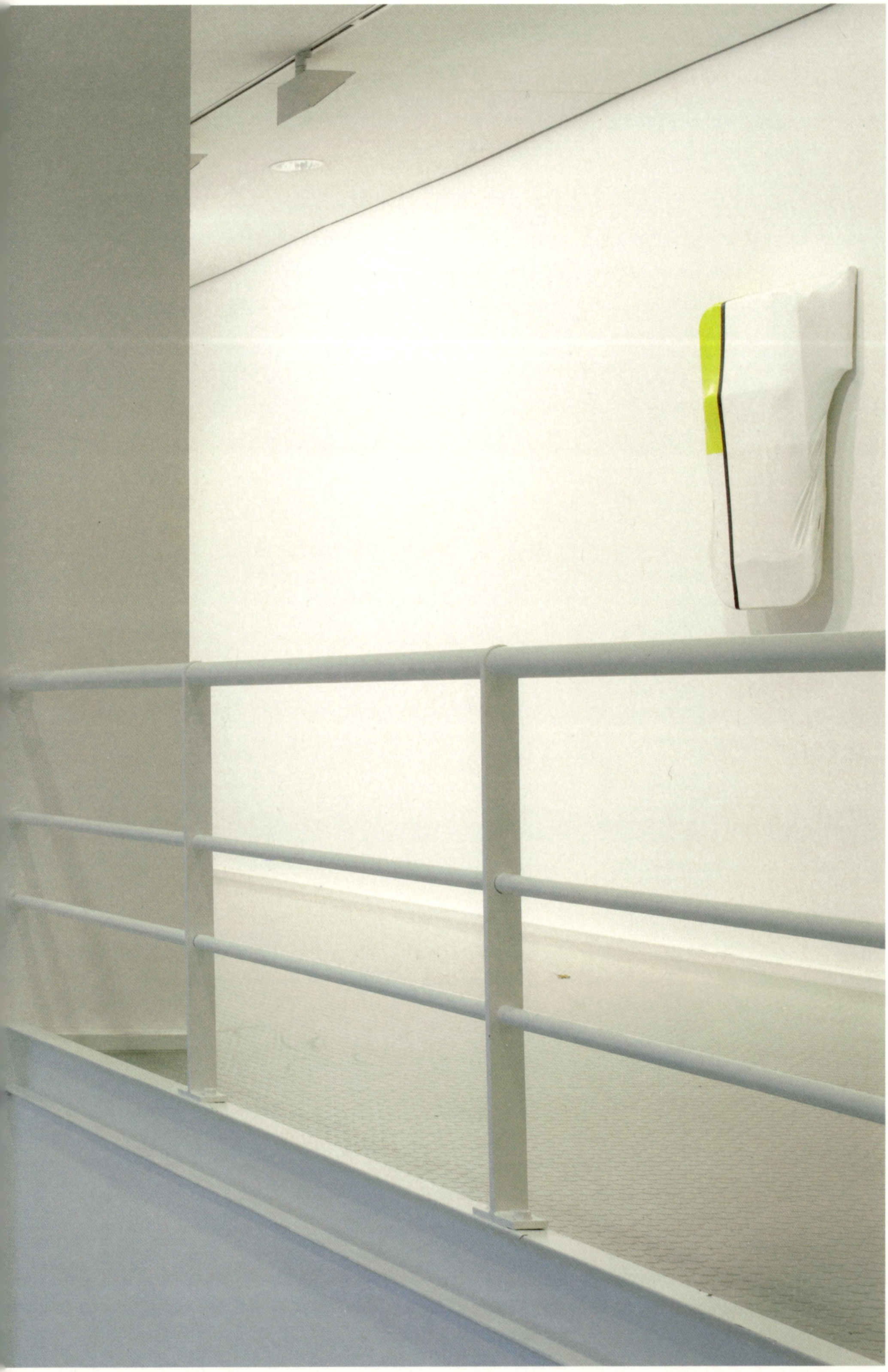

125

MARTÍN MELE – CURRICULUM VITAE

1960   Born in Buenos Aires, Argentina.
Lives and works in Düsseldorf and Buenos Aires.

SOLO EXHIBITIONS

2010   ›Das Archiv im Wurm / El Archivo en la Polilla / The Archive in the Worm‹
Argentina: Museo de Bellas Artes, Salta; Macro, Rosario; Museo de Arte Contemporáneo, Neuquén; Museo Marítimo, Ushuaia; Switzerland: Lokal-int, Biel; Germany: Atelierfrankfurt, Frankfurt; art forum berlin, Berlin; Kulturforum Alte Post, Neuss
Galerie Cosar EY5, Düsseldorf, Germany
Galerie Ebbers, Kranenburg, Germany

2008   ›Süße Alpträume‹, Field Institute, Raketenstation Hombroich, Germany
Performance, Langen Foundation, Germany
›Nose-sense‹, Galerie Mark Müller, Zürich, Switzerland
›Gestern und Heute‹, Malkasten, with Celina Jure, Düsseldorf, Germany

2007   ›Mele vs. Mele‹, Museo MACO, Oaxaca, México (C)
Kunstverein Aichach, Aichach, Germany
Performance, Kunstverein Arnsberg, Germany
Galeria Jacobo Karpio, San José, Costa Rica

2006   ›Hin und Zurück‹, Virtuell Visuell e.V, with Celina Jure, Dorsten, Germany (C)
Galería Alberto Sendrós, Buenos Aires, Argentina
›Handfest‹, Galerie Mark Müller, with Katharina Grosse, Zürich, Switzerland

2005   ›La revuelta de la pintura‹, Sala Rivadavia, Cadiz, Spain (C)
Galerie Helmut Doll, Euskirchen, Germany

2004   Fundación Proa, Buenos Aires; Argentina
›Mücken vor den Augen‹, Versandhalle, with David Zepter, Grevenbroich, Germany (C)

2003   ›Argentinische Birnen‹, Museum Baden, Solingen, Germany
›Argentinische Birnen‹, Delta Werk, Solingen, Germany
Galerie Christa Schübbe, Projectroom, Düsseldorf, Germany

2002   Museo de arte contemporáneo, Bahia Blanca, Buenos Aires, Argentina (C)

2001   ›von Menschenhand‹, Performance, Museum Baden, Solingen, Germany

2000   Zugweg, Köln, Germany (C)
Performance, Onomato, Düsseldorf, Germany

GROUP EXHIBITIONS

2010   ›above realism‹, Galerie Cosar HMT, Düsseldorf, Germany

2009   ›Sugar babies‹, Galerie Ebbers, Kranenburg, Germany

2008   ›No country‹, Galerie Ebbers, Kranenburg, Germany

2006   ›For Painters in a Tree‹, Galerie Appel, Frankfurt, Germany

2004   ›Das erinnerte Haus‹, Folkwang Museum, Essen, Germany

2003   Städtische Galerie, Viersen, Germany

2002   ›Die Hafenlichtspiele-Rolle‹, Düsseldorf, Germany

2001   Southfirst gallery, Brooklyn, N.Y., USA
›Freie Wahlen‹, Kunsthalle Baden-Baden, Germany
›Argentinier im Spiegel‹, Goethe Institut Berlin, Germany (C)
›Trendwände‹, Kunstraum Düsseldorf, Germany

MARTÍN MELE – DAS ARCHIV IM WURM / EL ARCHIVO EN LA POLILLA / THE ARCHIVE IN THE WORM

Editor	Galerie Mark Müller, Zürich
Concept	Martín Mele, Taki Kiometzis
Texts	Andrés Duprat, Carl Friedrich Schröer, Raimund Stecker
Design	Taki Kiometzis/threehorses
Editing	Yasmin Afschar
Proof-Reading	Silvia Jaklitsch
Translations	Brian Currid (zweisprachkunst.de), Sonia Kirschstein, Christian Ebert
Photos	Lucia Bartolini, Hanna Brandt, Galerie Cosar HMT, Juan Carlos Gonzalez-Santiago, Heinrich Helfenstein, Celina Jure, Taki Kiometzis, Mara Monetti, Galerie Mark Müller, Martín Mele, Hans Willi Notthoff, Robert Schüll, Isodoro Zang
Reprographics	Taki Kiometzis/threehorses
Print	Druckstudio GmbH
Copyright	© 2011, Verlag für moderne Kunst Nürnberg, Martín Mele and the authors All right reserved Printed in Germany ISBN 978-3-86984-131-1

The publication was made possible through the great financial support of
Kunststiftung NRW, Galerie Mark Müller, Museo Marítimo Ushuaia, Kulturforum Alte Post, Secretaría de cultura de la Nación

Many thanks to
first of all Celina Jure, and all of you who helped me to realize this project: Yasmin Afschar, Corinna Bimboese, Michael Cosar, Sebastian Daub, Andrés Duprat, Christian Ebert, Andrea Elias, Chri Frautschi, Verónica Goycochea, Paula Jure, Virginia Jure, Mark Müller, Klaus Richter, Angelika Ritter, Julia Schmidt, Carl Friedrich Schröer, Cristina Sommer, Raimund Stecker, Nadja Thiel, Carlos Pedro Vairo, Maru Venanzi

Bibliographic information published by Die Deutsche Bibliothek
Die Deutsche Bibliothek lists this publication in the Deutsche Nationalbibliografie; detailed bibliographic data is available on the Internet at http//dnb.ddb.de.

Distributed in the United Kingdom
Cornerhouse Publications
70 Oxford Street, Manchester M1 5 NH, UK
phone +44-161-200 15 03, fax +44-161-200 15 04

Distributed outside Europe
D.A.P. Distributed Art Publishers, Inc.
155 Sixth Avenue, 2nd Floor, New York, NY 10013, USA
phone +1-212-627 19 99, fax +1-212-627 94 84